Ziran

SUNY series in Chinese Philosophy and Culture
―――――――――
Roger T. Ames, editor

Ziran

The Philosophy of Spontaneous Self-Causation

BRIAN BRUYA

Published by State University of New York Press, Albany

© 2022 State University of New York

All rights reserved

Printed in the United States of America

No part of this book may be used or reproduced in any manner whatsoever without written permission, with the exception of figure 3.4, which is from Wikimedia Commons, and is available under a Creative Commons license. No part of this book may be stored in a retrieval system or transmitted in any form or by any means including electronic, electrostatic, magnetic tape, mechanical, photocopying, recording, or otherwise
without the prior permission in writing of the publisher.

For information, contact State University of New York Press, Albany, NY
www.sunypress.edu

Library of Congress Cataloging-in-Publication Data

Name: Bruya, Brian, author.
Title: Ziran : The philosophy of spontaneous self-causation / Brian Bruya.
Description: Albany : State University of New York Press, [2022] | Series: SUNY series in Chinese Philosophy and Culture | Includes bibliographical references and index.
Identifiers: ISBN 9781438488318 (hardcover : alk. paper) | ISBN 9781438488325 (ebook) | ISBN 9781438488301 (pbk. : alk. paper)
Further information is available at the Library of Congress.

10 9 8 7 6 5 4 3 2 1

For
Yuling and Giorgio
boundless love

Contents

Acknowledgments	ix
Introduction	1
1. *Ziran* and Its Absence in Western Philosophy	7
2. Saving Natural Human Action from the Paradox of Spontaneity	37
3. Effortless Attention: A Missing Concept in Contemporary Cognitive Science	65
4. Broadening Aesthetics: Spontaneity, the Somatic Arts, and Improvisation	91
Epilogue	123
Notes	127
Works Cited	141
Index	145

Acknowledgments

I owe a debt of gratitude to the Collaborative Innovation Center of Confucian Civilization at Shandong University, where I was visiting scholar for the 2018–19 academic year and under whose auspices the first three chapters of this book were delivered as lectures. Yu Xiaoyu, with the help of Cui Xiang, expertly arranged all details of the lectures and their recording. Thanks also to Ma Aiju and Ye Da, who transcribed the lectures and translated them into Chinese for publication in China, the original intended audience of this book. And thanks to Kai Marchall and National Chengchi University's Research Center of Chinese Cultural Subjectivity in Taiwan, where a major portion of the fourth chapter was delivered as a lecture. Thanks to Roger Ames, who after writing a preface for the Chinese version, suggested that the book also be published in English. The English version was arranged and polished while I was on a Fulbright award as visiting professor at National Taiwan University's department of philosophy. Many thanks to Shandong University, Fulbright, NTU, and Eastern Michigan University for allowing me the time and resources to complete this project. I appreciate the close reading and detailed suggestions provided for the Chinese edition (which often made their way into the English edition) by Liu Chang (of People's Publishing House), Ma Aiju, and Ye Da and for the English edition by Sarah Mattice and an anonymous referee. The book is much better for their objections, corrections, and suggestions. Any remaining errors or oversights are due to my own limitations.

Thanks also to Bernhard Hommel for allowing me to use his illustration on p. 83 and to *Philosophy East and West* and MIT Press for allowing me to reproduce previously published material. The two brain illustrations in Figure 3.4 are labeled versions of images created by

Patrick J. Lynch and C. Carl Jaffe / CC-BY-2.5. The calligraphy on pp. 95–96 is from Xuanmi Pagoda Stele, as found in Guo Bonan (He Fei, tr.), *Gate to Chinese Calligraphy* (Beijing: Foreign Languages Press, 1996).

Introduction

A group of scientists in Seattle were trying to create a vaccine for the HIV virus, and they came across an enzyme that they thought might play a significant role. In microbiology, the shape of enzymes matters because they work like locks and keys. Therefore, the scientists needed to know the shape of this enzyme. They worked on it for a long time but couldn't figure out its exact shape, even after creating complex computer models of it. The project went on for ten years with no solution. Out of a sense of urgency, the scientists decided to open the project to the public to see if others could help. They took their computer models, put them in a game, and released the game publicly to video gamers. In three weeks, the video gamers had solved the puzzle.

Let's think about this for a moment. Microbiologists tend to be pretty smart people and are definitely specialists in their field. After ten years, they could not solve the puzzle of the shape of this enzyme. But video gamers were able to solve it in just three weeks. Is this because video gamers are smarter than scientists? Not necessarily. Let's look at a similar story about solving difficult problems.

Timothy Gowers is a celebrated mathematician. In 1998, he won the Fields Medal, which is like the Nobel Prize for mathematics. In the field of mathematics, there are many difficult problems that go back many decades. Very capable and very smart mathematicians have tried to solve these problems but have been unable to do so. Gowers decided to do what the scientists in Seattle did and invite the public to help with these long-standing problems. Terence Tao, another Fields Medal winner, joined the group, and many others, from college professors to high school math teachers to common hobbyists. One would think that Gowers and Tao, the two smartest mathematicians in the group, would have been able to solve the problems all by themselves, but it didn't turn out that way. Those two certainly made the majority of contributions, but it took contributions from a whole range of people to make progress. The group, called Polymath, solved some of the problems and at this writing has six publications in mathematics journals.

What we see in both of these examples is that some of the smartest people around could not solve very difficult problems on their own. And when they opened the process to a wider range of people, they suddenly made progress. Why? What happened? Why did adding more people yield better results than just having a small group of very smart people? Let's explore this question.

I found these two stories in the work of Scott Page, an economist and political scientist at the University of Michigan. He studies diversity, and he and Lu Hong, a mathematician, have used mathematics to demonstrate that diversity is more effective than sheer intelligence when trying to solve difficult problems. In other words, if you have ten of the smartest people in a room working on a difficult problem but they all come from more or less the same background, they will be less successful in solving the problem than ten less smart people of more diverse backgrounds. I think this is an important insight.

Page says that when we think about diversity, we usually think of identity diversity—gender, age, ethnicity, sexual orientation, etc. What matters most, though, is what he calls cognitive diversity. Cognitive diversity has two aspects, according to him: perspectives and heuristics. Perspectives are how we organize information in the world, classifying it, arranging it, associating some items and disassociating others. Heuristics are how we process the information that we have already organized in order to solve a problem. Heuristics are like a problem-solving toolbox.

As an example, suppose you are going up a hill and there is an obstacle in the road, such as a giant boulder. You wonder how to deal with the boulder and realize you have a hammer. You use the hammer to pound on the boulder, but it has little effect. Suppose there are nine other people with you, all with hammers like yours. Together you pound on the rock, but still it is largely unaffected. Now suppose ten people come up behind you. One of them has a hammer, but they also have many other tools, such as a portable drill, a rope, a crowbar, even a drone. With all of these different tools, the second group of ten will be more likely to solve the problem of the boulder; one of them might even think to use the hammer as a lever.

Identity diversity is not necessarily unrelated to cognitive diversity—in fact, increasing identity diversity often helps increase cognitive diversity—but they are also not necessarily related, so the emphasis for effective problem solving should be on cognitive diversity.[1]

In philosophy, we have many difficult problems to solve. In fact, that's what philosophers do—we find the hardest problems and we try to make progress on them, and not only in the field of philosophy. Philosophers cross over just about every boundary, working for example in health care ethics, in law, in biology, in physics, etc. We've been trying to solve difficult problems for hundreds of years. I think that we can use Page's insights to improve our problem-solving ability, not just in philosophy but across academia.

Let's think for a moment about how learning is constructed and organized in academia. Suppose you are a biologist. In your training, you are taught by your teachers to see problems as a biologist sees them. When you look at a living creature, you view it in terms of cells, tissues, organs, organ systems, species, etc. Why are you taught to view life this way? Because most of the time, it is the most effective way of making progress in biology. But now suppose you are faced with a long-standing problem that no biologist has been able to solve. In the end, it turns out that the best way to solve the problem was to view it in terms of information rather than cells and organs.

In physics, you are taught to see certain phenomena in terms of discrete bodies that bump into each other in law-like ways. Then some experimental results turn out to involve randomness. Now how should the phenomena you study be thought of?

In field after field, there are acceptable methods, which are really habits of thinking, beliefs about the best way to get results and make progress. In this sense, we are all indoctrinated into the dogmas of our fields, making it so that there is a lack of diversity in each field. This is why universities often promote interdisciplinary studies. They are trying to get people from different disciplines to talk to each other in order to catalyze new ideas.

Now consider where our disciplines come from. Every university is organized into fields of study: biology, physics, anthropology, literature, philosophy, etc. Each of these fields, along with universities themselves, arose in its modern sense in the West—in Europe and America. That means that as you are indoctrinated into your field within any university around the world, you are also indoctrinated into a way of thinking that has its roots in the West. Even if you were raised in China, when you study biology, you are taught to think like a biologist, and because biology arose in the West, it has naturally inherited certain assumptions going all the way back to the Ancient Greeks.

We are taught in high school that the scientific method is free of bias and so is free of unfounded assumptions. But this is naive. In order to do science well, as we've seen, one must approach every step in any field largely from the point of view of one's predecessors. No one can start over from scratch. We all inherit the assumptions of our teachers.

Now consider that in addition to what occurred in the West, in places such as China and India, great intellects have been thinking about problems of the human condition for thousands of years. Around the world, very smart people have been working on very difficult problems and have written down their results in what we now call literature, philosophy, religion, and history. This is a great reservoir of cognitive diversity—of perspectives and heuristics. But we throw all of that aside when we do biology, or physics, or sociology—even contemporary philosophy. The main claim in this book is that recovering some of these ancient insights can help us make progress in intellectual endeavors today—together, they can act as a new cognitive toolbox to help us with exceedingly difficult problems.

If Page is right that increasing cognitive diversity can help us solve difficult problems, and if ancient culture is a reservoir of cognitive diversity, then it only makes sense to study ancient culture and apply its perspectives and heuristics to problems today.

In what follows, I will give you concrete examples of this. I will show how I have taken a key idea from early Chinese philosophy and applied it to contemporary philosophy of action, cognitive science, and aesthetics. In each case, I will show how introducing the idea exposes some unseen assumptions in the field and helps us make progress in it. The point is not just to show how it might be possible to do this but how it has actually been done.

In chapter 1, I introduce the idea of *ziran* from early China. I explain in detail what it means in the context of early Chinese Daoism, then I canvass the Western philosophical tradition for close equivalents, showing why a number of seemingly good candidates are actually significantly different. I thus establish that the idea of *ziran* is a unique intellectual resource for topics of action, attention, and aesthetics. In chapter 2, I apply the idea of *ziran* to a long-standing paradox in Western philosophy and show how the paradox can be solved by introducing this idea and how the idea can help us make further progress in the philosophy of action. In chapter 3, I apply the idea of *ziran* to contemporary cognitive psychology, exposing hidden assumptions about attention and showing how the field has been advanced by introducing this idea. In chapter 4, I apply the concept of *ziran* to contemporary art and aesthetics, delineating a new kind of art and clarifying the notion of improvisation.[2]

This book is a transcription of talks given at Shandong University, China, and National Chengchi University, Taiwan. The talks were intended to be a unified and simplified statement of ideas that are already in print in several different publications. Their unity in one place in a less technical idiom allows the reader easier access to the project, which is to use the tools of comparative philosophy to import a significant intellectual resource from a premodern non-Western culture into the contemporary intellectual conversation. In creating and delivering the talks, I attempted to take the ordinarily complex and technical form of academic writing and strip it down to its bare essentials, to say only as much as necessary to make my points, with no complex elaborations or technical asides. The full publications from which the various chapters of this book are derived are mentioned in the final pages of the book. Readers are encouraged to turn to them for more detail.

Chapter 1

Ziran and Its Absence in Western Philosophy

Spontaneous Self-Causation, or Natural Action, in Daoism

Importing a concept from one tradition into another is challenging. Not only do the languages not exactly match up, neither do the conceptual schemes. When Catholic Jesuit missionaries first went to China and tried to explain their idea of God to the Chinese, translating God as *shangdi* 上帝 (the most obvious Chinese equivalent) didn't evoke the same associations as the term *Deus* did in Latin. Instead, they adopted a more obscure word—*tianzhu* 天主—so that they could infuse it with their own associations.[1]

In the first three chapters of this book, I import the ancient Chinese concept of spontaneous self-causation, or natural action, into contemporary thought. In the classical Chinese tradition, there were two basic terms for this: *ziran* 自然 and *wu wei* 無為.[2] I will often use *ziran*, or "spontaneity," as a blanket term for the idea.

The first step will be to explain the idea in its original context. To do this, I will run through three distinct ways of expressing it in classical Daoist texts—first, through the term *ziran*; second, through the term *wu wei*; finally, through the skill episodes in the *Zhuangzi*. After giving a full explanation of the idea in its original context, I will canvass the Western philosophical tradition for a robustly theorized equivalent idea. Spoiler alert: there is none. The closest we come prior to the twentieth century is the idea of spontaneity (from the Latin *sponte*). As the exploration unfolds, it will become clear why that idea is philosophically problematic.

Ziran 自然

At first glance, interpreting the Chinese word *ziran* 自然 seems easy and straightforward. It means *nature,* as in forests, streams, mountains, and sunsets, cranes migrating north and pandas munching on bamboo. But this is its meaning in contemporary Chinese. We are interested in its meaning in Classical Chinese, the Chinese of the Daoists Laozi and Zhuangzi[3] in particular, who lived in the first few centuries BCE.

In contemporary Chinese, most words have two characters. In Classical Chinese, most words have one character. So when we see a word such as 自然 from classical Chinese and want to understand exactly what it means, it helps to break it down and look at the characters separately. When we do this, we find that the term is actually quite complicated.

The meaning of the character *ran* 然 is itself difficult to pin down, as it functions in two related but distinct ways. When occurring by itself, it means *such as this* or *like this,* or just *such* or *this.* For example, chapter 77 of the *Laozi* describe the "*dao* of nature" and then says of the "*dao* of people," *bu ran* 不然—that it is not like this (i.e., it is different). The preposition *ranhou* 然後 (afterward/and then) in contemporary Chinese is derived from this meaning, combining *ran* 然 and *hou* 後 (after) to get *after such* (see *Laozi* 65). *Ran* occurs in this sense also in chapters 54 (吾何以知天下然哉, how do I know the world is like this?) and 57 (吾何以知其然哉, how do I know it is like this?).

Ran 然 also means something like *having the appearance of* or *being in a state of.* In this sense, it invariably occurs immediately following an adjective. We see an example of this in *Laozi* 26 *chao ran* 超然—aloof in appearance. It also appears in this sense in *Laozi* chapters 53 (*jie ran* 介然) and 73 (*chan ran* 繟然).

Outside of the above seven occurrences in the *Laozi,* the character *ran* 然 occurs five more times, all preceded by the character *zi* 自. As the second of two characters, it seems at first glance to also mean in these instances *having the appearance of* or *being in a state of.* But what does *zi* 自 mean?

If you ask a scholar of Classical Chinese grammar what *zi* 自 means, the first response you will get is probably something such as, "That's easy, it is a coverb meaning *action from.*" The following are examples in which the word *zi* carries the meaning *action from*:

自古及今 from the past up to the present (*Laozi* 21)[4]

自此以往 going on from here (*Zhuangzi* 2)

自吾執斧斤以隨夫子 since we took up our axes to follow you, sir (*Zhuangzi* 4)

自其同者視之 look at them from the viewpoint of their similarities (*Zhuangzi* 5)

The *zi* 自 of *ziran* 自然, however, cannot mean *action from*, otherwise the entire two-character term would mean something like *being in the state of from*, which wouldn't make much sense.

Another meaning of *zi* 自 is as a reflexive pronominal adverb, meaning *to do oneself* or *to do for oneself*. For instance:

自謂 to refer to oneself (*Laozi* 39)

自遺其咎 bring tragedy upon themselves (*Laozi* 9)

自知者明 to know oneself is acuity (*Laozi* 33)

自事其心者 in service to one's own mind (*Zhuangzi* 4)

不能自解者 cannot free oneself from bonds (*Zhuangzi* 6)

This seems like a more useful way of understanding *zi* 自 for our purposes. One example that seems at first glance to also fit this pattern is in the phrase *min zi zheng* 民自正, which under this construal would mean *the people correct themselves*. Interestingly, however, that is not how translators tend to render it. Here are two translations from well-known Chinese scholars:

The people of themselves become correct.[5]

The people are rectified of themselves.[6]

What do the translators mean by "of themselves"?

Let's call the first interpretation ("the people correct themselves") the *typical* interpretation of *zi,* and let's call the "of themselves" rendering the *special* interpretation of *zi.* In the typical interpretation, there is a discrete subject, a discrete object, and the subject is doing something to the object. In this example, the subject and object happen to be the same. The form of the sentence under this interpretation is that there is an action, and one is doing the action to oneself. There is a subject/object dichotomy, there is intentionality, and there is a clear path of causation.

What about the special interpretation of *zi*: "the people of themselves become correct"? This is a very different way of saying that something is happening. There is no directionality to it. There is no intentionality to it. And there is no subject/object dichotomy.

What I'm suggesting is that the special interpretation is the proper understanding of the *zi* 自 of *ziran* 自然. There is an emphasis on the impetus over the effect. Thus, it is not that the people are correcting themselves. Rather, it is that the people are becoming correct, and nobody outside is doing it to them. It's just happening. There is a softening of causation away from a single impetus deliberateness to what I call a more vague multivalent causation. The same chapter has three more examples of this usage. Here are all four together:

我無為，而民自化；

我好靜，而民自正；

我無事，而民自富；

我無欲，而民自樸.

I take no action and the people are transformed of themselves;

I prefer stillness and the people are rectified of themselves;

I am not meddlesome and the people prosper of themselves;

I am free from desire and the people of themselves become simple like the uncarved block.

To get a better sense of the distinction between these two understandings of causation, consider the following two sentences in plain English:

The universe moves itself

The universe moves *of* itself.

In the first, there is the universe as the subject, there is the universe as the object, and the universe is doing something to itself. Now, consider the second one. It is a very different sense. All we really know is that the universe is moving and nobody's doing it to the universe. It's just happening. This is the sense of *zi* 自 in *ziran* 自然. There is no presupposition regarding a self, causation, or the relationship. Something is just happening and there is a self somehow involved in initiating it.

The word *zi* 自 occurs many times across the *Laozi* and *Zhuangzi*. It occurs seventeen times in this sense, and half of them are in the term *ziran*, but half of them are not. This sense of *zi* is what I want to point out as a unique idea in the philosophy of action stemming from the early Daoist tradition. We can define it as *movement, or action, from internal resources, with no interference, in a multivalent causality*. Like many philosophers around the world, the Daoists were trying to account for movement and changes that we see in the world. They wanted to know: When things move in the world, how do we make sense of that movement? Where does it come from? What are its effects? What can we say about the process?

What we are talking about in technical terms is *self-causation*, and the best English term for this kind of self-causation is *spontaneity*. To understand the idea of *zi* as spontaneous self-causation, I like to think of the example of a seed. If I take a seed and put it right here on the desk and say, "Grow!" it is not going to listen to me, even if I threaten it. I cannot force it to grow. But if I put it in its natural environment (moist, warm soil), it will *ziran*—it will grow of its own accord. It will grow from its own resources. Then it will connect to its environment, and the objective boundaries of the seed—what we might call its self—will blur in that connection. So you don't have the very clear sense of a discrete, enduring individual here (this latter point will become important later on).

We can easily see now why the contemporary sense of nature—mountains, forests, etc.—is not an appropriate sense of *ziran* in the early period. However, the adverb *naturally* seems to work better, as it has a sense of a process growing out of itself. And the adjective *natural* can work when paired with *motion* or *action*.

In the 1970s in the West, the biologists Humberto Maturana and Francisco Verala felt that there was no good term for describing the processes of nature unfolding and self-creating, so they proposed a new word: *autopoiesis*, which derives from the Greek and means *to self-create*. I think this is very close to the idea of *ziran*. The English word *spontaneity* derives from the Latin *sponte*, which means *self-caused*. Unfortunately, in colloquial English, it can also mean *impulsive*, so if we use it as a technical translation of *ziran*, the meaning must be specified.

Wu Wei 無為

So far, we have looked at the term *ziran* to get at this special notion of self-causation from Daoism. There are two more ways to get at it. The second way is through *wu wei* 無為, which literally means an absence of action and is often translated *non-action*. We find the term in both the *Laozi* and *Zhuangzi*. Consider the following passages:

> Do *wu wei* and everything is governed 為無為，則無不治 (*Laozi* 3)

> Dao always *wu wei*, and everything gets done 道常無為而無不為 (*Laozi* 37)

> Lessening and lessening, until finally reaching *wu wei* 損之又損，以至於無為 (*Laozi* 48)

> I *wu wei*, and the people transform spontaneously 我無為，而民自化 (*Laozi* 57)

> The sage *wu wei*, and for this reason nothing is ruined 聖人無為故無敗 (*Laozi* 64)

In the first passage, we see a description of how a leader governs. The leader doesn't do a whole lot, and yet everything gets done. In the second, we see a description of how the Dao functions—that is, of how the processes of nature function. There's not a lot of intentional action going on, but everything that needs to get done gets done. The third passage describes a psychological state. We come to university to fill our heads full of information, but *Laozi* said that if we empty ourselves, we can get closer to this process of *wu wei*. In the fourth passage, we see a leader again. Notice that this is the source of *zi hua* 自化 and *zi zheng* 自正 that we saw above. Because of the leader's *wu wei*, the people transform of their own accord. Here, we see a direct connection between *zi* 自 and *wu wei*. I am suggesting that these two terms represent fundamentally the same idea.

Both *ziran* and *wu wei* can refer to motion in nature broadly and in individuals specifically, but *ziran* tends to be used more often in the former sense and *wu wei* in the latter sense. As such, we can define *wu wei* in the following way: *action that is absent direct intentionality*.[7] So, again, things are happening, but I'm not trying to do it. I'm not doing it with effort. I'm not doing it artificially. And yet everything that needs to happen is happening.

There are two basic ways to understand *wu wei*. The first is in terms of a leader who is so effective in his leadership that people do what needs to be done without being asked or ordered. In this sense, it is very close to the idea of actually doing nothing, but of course in order to get the people to voluntarily do what needs to be done, much work must go into establishing policy and setting an example. The causal pathway is, therefore, indirect, and there is no direct intentionality leading from the leader wanting to accomplish *x* and *x* being accomplished. That is why it is characterized as *wu wei*.

The second way of understanding *wu wei* as action absent direct intentionality is through a specific action that occurs without *trying*. When I was in the eighth grade, I was a pitcher for our school baseball team. I wasn't a very good pitcher, and to help me improve, the coach told me to throw the ball to the catcher's mitt without *aiming* at the catcher's mitt—an idea that eluded me at the time ("If I don't aim for the mitt, how can I hit it?" I thought to myself). This sense of an absence of intentionality has to do with an absence of artificiality and effort. We can get a better understanding of this second sense of *wu wei* through the skill episodes of the *Zhuangzi*.

The Skill Episodes of the *Zhuangzi*

The third way to get at the idea of spontaneous self-causation, or natural action, from Daoism is through specific episodes in the *Zhuangzi*.

There are quite a few stories of people who have particular skills in the *Zhuangzi*. Many of them are in chapter 19.[8] Toward the beginning of the chapter, we see this line:

> With one's body whole and one's energy restored, become one with nature. 夫形全精复，与天为一

This appears to be a preface to the stories that follow. It suggests that the stories describe a process of becoming one with *tian* 天, the term in the classical period for *nature*, as in mountains, forests, etc., but still with a key element being its processes, its unfolding movement.[9] When you achieve a high level of a particular skill, you are achieving a natural level of ability, which is the highest level of an ability. For a Daoist, to become more and more like nature is to be a better and better person. The ideal kind of action is natural action.

There are many skill stories in the *Zhuangzi*. We'll look at just four, each of which will be used to represent one distinct aspect of Daoist natural action.

The first story is about a cicada catcher. In this story, a man is out collecting cicadas with a long pole, and he is very good at it. Confucius sees him doing this and, impressed, asks about his method. "First," the man says, "I try to balance two balls on the tip of my pole. When I can do that, I know I am almost ready." Next, he tries to balance three balls on top of his pole. When he can do that, he tries to balance five balls. When he is finally able to do that, he knows that he's ready to really concentrate. And here is how he describes his state of concentration: "Despite the expansiveness of the world and the multitude of things in it, all I see are the cicada wings, and nothing else can distract me from them. 雖天地之大，萬物之多，而唯蜩翼之知." Thus, we see in this episode the importance of a high level of concentration in accomplishing natural action. This is one of the psychological aspects of human *ziran,* or *wu wei.*[10]

In the second illustrative episode, there is a fellow who makes wooden stands for racks of bells and chimes used in ceremonies. He is so good at it and has such a good reputation that the ruler of the state of Lu takes an interest and asks him how he does it. He replies, "When I build a bell stand, I don't want to exhaust my energies. So first I fast. After fasting for three days, I have dismissed all thought of payment or reward. After five days. I have no fears of ruining my reputation due to poor craftsmanship. After seven days, I have dismissed all awareness of my own body. 臣將為鐻，未嘗敢以耗氣也，必齊以靜心。齊三日，而不敢懷慶賞爵祿；齊五日，不敢懷非譽巧拙；齊七日，輒然忘吾有四枝形體也." This is an example of getting rid of things, as we saw in a previous quotation from *Laozi*. He is getting rid even of the sense of his own body, of his own self. So there remains only the activity. That is when he feels ready to go out into the forest to find the trees that will suit the construction of a bell stand. There is no good English word for this process. The best I can find is to call it *letting go*, or shedding—that is, getting rid of unnecessary things.

In a third episode, there is a fellow who dives into roiling water, where it looks as if nobody would be able to safely swim. Confucius sees him dive in and mistakenly thinks he is committing suicide. When the swimmer emerges from the water, Confucius asks about his method. The swimmer says that he doesn't have a special method, continuing: "It's second nature for me. I go in with the eddies and out with the swells, following the flow of the water instead of my own inclinations. 吾始乎故，長乎性，成乎命。與齊俱入，與汩偕出，從水之道而不為私焉." The swimmer doesn't have time to stop and think, "What should I do?" He has to respond immediately to whatever is happening. This is what I call *responsiveness,* and it is a third aspect of *wu wei,* or *ziran.*

The fourth episode also involves a swimmer. His swimming is described in this way: "A good swimmer forgets the water. 善游者數能，忘水也." In other words, it is experienced with a feeling of ease or the absence of a feeling of difficulty. This is the fourth aspect of *wu wei,* or *ziran*—that instead of feeling difficult, it feels easy, even though it involves a very high level of skill. This idea is also implicit in the other three episodes. Catching cicadas, making bell stands, and swimming in roiling water are difficult to do well, but under the right circumstances of concentration, letting go, and responsiveness, the activities can be engaged in such a way that they don't *feel* difficult.

To summarize, the four aspects of Daoist natural action that we find in these four episodes are:

- Concentration—a high level of attention within a single domain of activity

- Letting go—getting rid of thoughts and feelings not germane to the activity

- Responsiveness—being able to respond quickly and accurately
- Ease—being able to execute a complex, demanding activity with a subjective feeling of effortlessness

The first two can be grouped into one category—namely, *wholeness*, a reference to the holistic, unfractured nature of this psychological state. The last two can be grouped under the rubric of *fluency*, a reference to the manner of the action.

Although I have used only four episodes to elucidate the above four ideas, the ideas occur repeatedly across skill stories in the *Zhuangzi*, which occur in as many as 16 episodes in 9 different chapters. Together, they help us get a clear understanding of skill in *Zhuangzi* and thus of *wu wei*, or *ziran*.

We have now examined Daoist natural action, or spontaneous self-causation, from three perspectives. From examining the term *zi* 自, we uncovered the idea of action that arises from internal resources, without interference, and that occurs through multivalent causality. From examining the term *wu wei*, we found that this kind of action is absent direct intentionality. From examining the skill episodes in *Zhuangzi*, we found that this kind of action involves wholeness (concentration and letting go) and fluency (responsiveness and ease).

Spontaneous Self-Causation, or Natural Action, in the Western Tradition

In examining passages from the *Laozi* and *Zhuangzi*, I posited that there is a single kind of action in Daoist theory that can be understood from three different perspectives. In what follows, we turn to five Western philosophers to see if we can find an equivalent idea.

Before we do that, let's stop and think about what exactly the Daoists are claiming. Number one, they have a descriptive theory. In other words, they are saying, in reference to this idea of action: this is how things are in the world—there is a kind of action that we can describe in the way we've described it thus far. But that is not all they are saying. They also have a prescriptive theory, meaning that they are claiming that this kind of action is the preferred kind of action—it is best to be natural.[11]

One way that the work of philosophers differs from the work of intellectual historians is that not only are we philosophers interested in the history of ideas, we also ask if the ideas are true and whether they are still relevant today.[12] So, now we are faced with two claims from the Daoists:

1. There is a kind of movement in the world that we can call spontaneous self-causation, or natural action (*ziran*).

2. It is the preferred kind of action for human beings.

Are these claims true? I submit that claim number one is true—there is a kind of movement in the world that can accurately be characterized in this way. What about claim number two?

Confucius said, "At the age of seventy, I could act according to my wishes without overstepping boundaries 七十而從心所欲不逾矩" (*Analects*, 2.4). According to Confucius, there is a whole lot of work that goes into the back end of getting actions just right, but when it happens, it can happen with great facility. It can come off as easy. From this perspective, it seems as though Confucius would agree. Even Xunzi, who advocated *wei* 為 (artifice) said:

When a person of *ren* puts the Dao into action, it is *wu wei*. 仁者之行道也，無為也.

In the early Chinese tradition, even among Confucians, there seems to have been a widely held belief that natural action is the ideal type of action. I won't venture my own opinion on the matter, but I raise the issue because it is worth thinking more about. As we shall see, Western philosophers have tended to dismiss the idea all too quickly.

Below, I shall discuss eight distinct candidates (four from one philosopher and one each from four others) from the Western tradition that approximate a Daoist idea of spontaneous self-causation, or natural action. Our job for each will be to determine how close it comes to being the same idea. To do this, we'll need to keep in mind the definition established above.

Aristotle

Let's begin with a passage from Aristotle:

> The difference between *automaton* and luck is greatest in things that come to be by *physis*; for when anything comes to be contrary to *physis*, we do not say that it came to be by luck but by *automaton*. (Physics 197b304–336)[13]

Key words are intentionally left untranslated. Even without understanding all of the words, you can get a sense that what Aristotle is trying to do here is account for different kinds of occurrences in the world. We see that *automaton* has something to do with luck, but it is somehow distinct. Here is a fuller translation:

> The difference between *spontaneity* and luck is greatest in things that come to be by *physis*; for when anything comes to be contrary to *physis*, we do not say that it came to be by luck but by *spontaneity*.

As you can see, *automaton* is translated into English as *spontaneity*. I said above that spontaneity might also be a good translation of *ziran*, so here we have a candidate for an equivalent notion of *ziran* in the West.

A crude way of doing comparative philosophy is to just to look for this kind of linguistic similarity. If a word from foreign language A is translated into the target language using a particular term, and a word from foreign language B is translated into the target language using the same term, our first intuition would be that the two different foreign language words represent the same concept. But to do comparative philosophy well, we have to be more careful than this. Let me give you a quick example to explain why.

The Greek word *eros* can be translated into English as *love*. The Chinese word *ren* can also be translated into English as *love*. Neither of these translations is an outright mistake, but to conclude that *eros* and *ren* therefore represent the same concept would be a grave error. *Eros* means sexual love and is distinct in Greek thought from *philia* (brotherly love) and *caritas* (expansive love). *Ren*, at least according to the *Analects* of Confucius, refers to a kind of top-down care for others that also involves a kind of expertise in social relations. There is no exact equivalent of *eros* in Chinese nor of *ren* in Greek. To force an equivalence where there is none would be to introduce confusion into the conceptual scheme of the respective philosophical system. In doing comparative philosophy, we have to be particularly careful of our word choices and examine whether anything is lost or accidentally added when we translate a technical philosophical term into another language. This is why it helps to first examine an idea in its original context, as we did above with *ziran* and *wu wei*.

Let's get back to Aristotle. It is true that *automaton* is often translated into English as *spontaneity*, and it was even translated into Latin as *sponte*, but Aristotle himself defines it in this context as something that happens contrary to the usual, unexpectedly, rarely—an aberration. The example he gives is a falling rock that unexpectedly hits someone on the head. Therefore, although *automaton* may be translated into English as *spontaneity*, and *ziran* may be translated into English as *spontaneity*, *automaton* (as Aristotle uses it here) and *ziran* do not remotely represent the same idea. *Automaton* refers merely to something anomalous that happens. That's a long way from being the highest form of skilled action, as in Daoism.

So we can cross *automaton* off the list of prospective candidates of ideas in the West that approximate the idea of Daoist natural action. *Automaton*, although it has an equivalent translation in English, does not come close to conceptually being the same as *ziran*.

There are four candidates for natural action in Aristotle. The second is *physis*. To understand *physis*, we can go back to the same quotation above:

> The difference between *automaton* and luck is greatest in things that come to be by *physis*; for when anything comes to be contrary to *physis*, we do not say that it came to be by luck but by *automaton*.

Physis is often translated into English as *nature*. So again, we have a lexical candidate for *ziran*, which we found above could be translated into English as *naturally* or *natural* (but not as *nature*). In his examination of motion, Aristotle says that inanimate objects are moved in two possible ways, either by force or by *physis* (nature). Consider the pen in my hand. The pen is not going to move by itself. I have to move it. Now I'm moving the pen in the air from right to left, and there it goes. It was moved by my force. That's what Aristotle means by *force*. But if the pen is allowed to fall, that's *physis*. That's nature. The pen, according to Aristotle, because it is a solid object, has a natural tendency to go down but requires a catalyst. Consider a hot air balloon. It has a tendency to go up. You catalyze it by letting it go, and it goes. You can say the same about pushing a rock over a cliff. The motion is directed by the nature of the object itself. That's what Aristotle means by *physis*. Is this the same as *ziran*? If not, what is the difference?

There are two possible answers to this question. One is: no, it's not the same, because in *physis* the object has to be catalyzed from the outside, whereas part of the basic definition of *ziran* is that there is no external factor involved—the motion happens "of itself." Another reason that *physis* is not the same as *ziran* is a bit more complicated, and it has to do with what we mean by *self*. Aristotle talks about the self as *psyche*—the soul or the mind, which involves desire, imagination, and intellect. Nothing in nature has a self, for Aristotle, unless it has a *psyche*. Only something with a *psyche* can move itself, but that involves a distinct subject/object dichotomy, whereas with *ziran*, when something moves "of itself," there is no such dichotomy. Thus, there are two reasons to think that *physis* is importantly distinct from *ziran*.

There is another way of answering this question though, which is: maybe. Maybe there is one way of looking at this issue in which it turns out that *physis* does approximate the basic notion of *ziran*. Consider the following passage from Aristotle:

> The man who has just become a scientist immediately begins investigating unless something prevents him. (*Physics* 8)[14]

Setting aside the word *scientist* here, which is an awkward translation of a word that means something more like *knower*, this sounds quite similar to Daoist natural action. Somebody is able to do something and just goes off and does it. They don't think about it ahead of time. It just happens. But now notice which text this comes out of. It comes out of Aristotle's *Physics*, which is an account of natural movement, not human movement. This particular example is actually very strange to see in this particular book. Scholars have also pointed out that this description of human movement in the *Physics* is actually contrary to descriptions of human movement in books such as the *Nicomachean Ethics*.[15] So even though this seems like Aristotle is saying something quite similar to *Laozi*, he doesn't develop it theoretically at all. In fact, it is contrary to a theory that he does develop elsewhere. So, unfortunately, we have to set this aside and say: No, *physis* is not what we are looking for, either.

The third candidate in Aristotle is *hexis,* and this is how we can define it: any action performed by an individual disposes that person to performing that action again under similar circumstances. This should sound familiar to a modern mind because the idea is still with us—it is the idea of habit.

The example of *hexis* that Aristotle gives is playing a musical instrument. As you learn how to play a musical instrument, it becomes easier and easier to do it. We can see this in the skill episodes of *Zhuangzi.* In building their skills, the cicada catcher, the carpenter, and the swimmers depend on habit. It is an important concept for Aristotle because he views virtues as habits.

The way Aristotle sees human psychology is that there is sort of a battle going on inside us. According to Aristotle, we have tendencies, such as desires and emotions, that do not necessarily engender good behavior. And so we develop virtues to counterbalance them, to do the right thing at the right time. Suppose I encounter a skirmish on a battlefield. My first inclination, motivated by fear, would be to run away from it. But if I were to develop the virtue of bravery, I could overcome my fear, and instead run toward the battle. It is in this sense, Aristotle says, that habits are important for human action. Is this the same thing as what we saw in *Zhuangzi* and *Laozi*? It is similar, but there are important differences, which you can see in Table 1.1.

In Daoist natural action, you have concentration on a particular activity. This narrows one's field of view to just that activity. Your considerations are concrete, narrow, in the moment. Remember the

Table 1.1. Aristotle's *hexis* in comparison with *ziran*

DAOIST NATURAL ACTION AS IDEAL ACTION	ARISTOTLE'S RATIONAL DELIBERATION + HABIT AS IDEAL ACTION
Concentration (focus on domain)	Rational deliberation (abstraction)
Letting go (toward vagueness)	Combating (toward clarity)
Responsiveness (drawn into force of circumstances)	Escape from force of circumstances
Ease—inner calm	Inner battle

cicada catcher focused only on the wings of the cicada? Aristotle, on the contrary, prefers slow, rational deliberation to determine whether an action is good or bad. One part of rational deliberation involves abstraction, away from the concrete, toward theory that can be applied in different circumstances at different times. It is quite different from a momentary focus on a particular domain.

In Daoism, you shed unwanted distractions, such as certain desires and emotions. As this occurs, there is a sense of melding with one's surroundings. Remember the seed that loses its boundaries as it grows? In Aristotle, there is a sense of combatting or suppressing such desires and emotions. To do this, one needs to clarify one's rational principles and assert one's individuality as a rational thinker.

In Daoist action, you also want to develop a kind of responsiveness such that you are drawn into the circumstances. In Aristotle, as we saw, he wants you to be able to abstract out from the circumstances and be free from their constraints. Theory is timeless.

Finally, for the Daoist, there is a sense of ease in the moment. For Aristotle, there is an inner battle. Aristotle does prize a kind of internal peace (*eudaimonia*), but he does not associate it with action in the moment.

We see, then, that even though there seems to be a lot of crossover between *hexis* and *ziran,* it is not a perfect fit. *Hexis* as habit is relevant to both philosophies insofar as it is necessary for skill development, but that is just a preliminary part of action for both of them. After skill development, the two philosophies diverge in multiple ways.

The fourth and final candidate in Aristotle is the *practical syllogism*. Before we get to the practical syllogism, per se, let's first review what a syllogism is. A syllogism is an argument of a particular form that includes a major premise and a minor premise. Consider the following argument:

All students are smart.

Tingting is a student.

Therefore, Tingting is smart.

The first line is the major premise, which is a general principle. The second line is the minor premise, which states a particular instance relevant to the general principle. The conclusion applies the general principle to the particular instance to come to a conclusion about the particular. It was Aristotle who discovered this logical form, known today as a syllogism.

In a practical syllogism the conclusion, instead of being a statement, is an action. For example:

All students go to eat dinner at 6:00 p.m. [major premise]

Tingting is a student. [minor premise]

[Action by Tingting of going to eat.] [conclusion]

Tingting thinks through the major premise and minor premise, and reaching the conclusion, simply goes to eat dinner. That's the practical syllogism—an action develops immediately, without thinking about it.

Here are two examples that Aristotle gives:

You conceive that every man ought to walk.

You are a man.

You immediately walk.

I ought to create a good.

A house is a good.

I immediately create a house.

Explaining, Aristotle says:

> Straightaway one [part] acts and the other responds. And on this account thinking that one ought to go and going are virtually simultaneous unless there be something else to hinder action. . . . The simultaneity and speed are due to the natural correspondence of the active and the passive. (*On the Motion of Animals* 8)

This kind of immediate action that bypasses extended deliberation seems similar to the kind of in-the-moment action that we have discussed in Daoism. Further, consider this passage from Aristotle:

> And the animal organism must be conceived after the similitude of a well-governed commonwealth. When order is once established in it there is no more need of a separate monarch to preside over each several task. The individuals each play their assigned part as is ordered, and one thing follows another in its accustomed order. (*On the Motion of Animals* 10)

This sounds just like Laozi. When Laozi talks about a good government, he says that everything just happens. It is unnecessary for the king to order people to do something. People just do it of their own accord. That is, coincidentally, the metaphor that Aristotle is using to describe the animal organism. Despite the similarity with Laozi, notice one thing: both of these passages from Aristotle come from a book called *On the Motion of Animals*. They are pertinent to animal movement, not to human movement. By contrast, here is an example Aristotle gives in the *Nicomachean Ethics* of the practical syllogism.

> Sweet things ought to be tasted.
>
> Yonder is a sweet thing.
>
> You immediately taste it. (*Nicomachean Ethics* 7)

The reason Aristotle brings up the practical syllogism in the *Nicomachean Ethics* is to explain unrestrained action. This is what a child would do, not what an adult human would do.

We might conclude that the practical syllogism looks a lot like *ziran*, but for Aristotle it is considered a lower form of action. The Daoists, in contrast, say that *ziran* is the highest form of action, the best way of acting.

After comparing four candidates for natural action in Aristotle (see Table 1.2 for a summary), we see that although there are intriguing linguistic and conceptual parallels, none is a close equivalent. In Daoist natural action, nature is the ideal model for action, but for Aristotle, nature represents unrestrained action. Aristotle wants to get away from nature. He prefers deliberation. But deliberation for Daoists is debilitating. If the swimmer in the roiling water stops to think, he will drown. For Aristotle, deliberation is the only path to the good. For a Daoist, natural action is conceived as the best path to achieving optimal results. So if a Daoist wants to engage in an activity, the best way to do it is *ziran*. For Aristotle, human action is conceived as achieving an ethical good specifically. So when Aristotle describes human action, he describes it in the context of ethics specifically.[16]

Aristotle is one of the most important philosophers in the history of Western philosophy. Alfred North Whitehead once said that all of Western philosophy is footnotes to Plato. But in the philosophy of action, which is what we are discussing, all of Western philosophy is footnotes to Aristotle. By pulling human beings away from nature in this way, Aristotle created a dichotomy that has baffled philosophers in Europe for two thousand years. As his ideas developed (and even in his own time), there was a sense that the way nature works is deterministic, that everything happens according to unbreakable laws. When I drop this pen, it goes down. If I drop it twenty times, it will go down twenty times. When I hold it up the twenty-first time and ask you, "Will this go down?" You'll say, "Yes, I know it will go down. It's a law of nature." But according to some of the heirs of Aristotle, humans are somehow able to break free from nature, toward ideal action.

Why was it so important for Aristotle and his heirs that human beings be able to break free from nature? Suppose you are standing in an elevator facing the closed door on your way up to your destination. The door opens to your floor, and you feel a hand on your back and

Table 1.2. *Ziran* vs. Aristotelian action

DAOIST SPONTANEITY	ARISTOTLE'S ACTION
Nature as the ideal model of action	Nature represents unrestrained action
Deliberation is debilitating	Deliberation leads to the good
Action conceived as achieving optimal results	Action conceived as achieving the ethical good
Spontaneity is the highest form of action	Spontaneity is a lower form of action

then a shove. How would you feel? A little bit angry? Now, suppose you're walking outside, and a small tree branch falls on you. Will you be angry at the tree? No. The reason for this, according to Western action theorists, is that the movement of the tree is determined, while the movement of a human being is free. And with freedom comes responsibility. This is what's so important to Aristotle. Without freedom, we cannot blame anybody for doing something wrong. And this is how it has been for the whole history of Western action theory from Aristotle.

You have to have freedom in order to have responsibility. At the same time, everything in nature is deterministic. So humans have to be different from nature. We're not natural. Human action cannot be natural, otherwise you cannot have responsibility. This created a huge problem philosophically.[17]

Aristotle's intellectual heirs adopted this dichotomy and struggled to reconcile human freedom with natural determinism. Epicurus took one path, suggesting that human action is outside of the natural order, it is *spontaneous*. He was an atomist and said that human spontaneity can be attributed to something he called "atomic swerve." Later on, Lucretius, an Epicurean, advanced this idea but referred to human action using the Latin term *libera voluntas*—free will. This is the earliest explicit mention of the idea of free will. Aristotle never mentioned free will per se, but the argument could be made that the idea is implicit in his philosophy. This is free will as spontaneity. Nothing is forcing you to do something. You are doing it from your own internal resources.

The Stoic philosopher Chrysippus took a different approach. He said that human action, like all the rest of nature, is deterministic. When we act, he said, we merely assent to natural impulses as they arise. Interestingly, he also used the term *spontaneous* to refer to this version of determined action. So, in the West, we have this strange situation where very early on human action was conceived as free by one school of thought and as determined by another school of thought, but both used the term *sponte*[18] to describe their view. I call this the paradox of spontaneity—one word that applies to contradictory accounts of movement. One kind is spontaneous as being freely willed, and the other kind is spontaneous as being determined by nature. This paradox has persisted for two thousand years. It persists even today.

Here is the problem. You know and I know, just like Darwin knew, that human beings are natural creatures. We evolved from earlier primates, after all. And yet, if we are truly free, then we cannot be entirely natural, if to be natural is to be determined. This is a problem that philosophers are still wrestling with—we have to be natural, but we cannot be natural. How do we make sense of this? What I am suggesting is that the word *spontaneous* gets used in both instances, and philosophers have never really noticed this. The paradox of spontaneity is a symptom of what is wrong with Western philosophy of action. We will address this problem directly in chapter 2.

When we look for approximations of Daoist natural action in the West, we will continually come across this issue. Looking closely at what philosophers mean by their use of the term *spontaneity* will allow us to get a sense of what the key differences are between Western theory of action and Chinese theory of action.

Julian Offray de La Mettrie

What does it mean for a human to be natural? Julian Offray de la Mettrie (1709–1751) was a physician in France who also considered himself a philosopher. He wrote a theory of human action, in which he referred to human action as *spontaneous*. According to his theory, there are three particular notions relevant to human action.

1. Nature is uniform, meaning that there are no exceptions to the laws of nature. Whatever laws there are apply to everything, including humans.

2. Matter moves of its own accord.

3. The mind is:

    a) Physical, specifically meaning that it is not spiritual. There is no spirit-matter dichotomy. Everything is material, including the mind.

    b) Unitary, meaning that there is no second aspect to it—such as a spiritual aspect—that is outside of the laws of nature.

    c) Sensitive, meaning that instead of rational deliberation, the primary function of the mind is feeling and responding.

I suggest that there is nothing here that contradicts *Laozi* or *Zhuangzi*. Everything is consistent with the Daoist notion of natural action.

According to what we discussed above, in the theory of Daoist action, nature is uniform, matter moves of its own accord, and the mind is physical,[19] unitary, and more about sensitivity and responsiveness than about rational deliberation.

So it seems that we have found in La Mettrie an example in the West that approximates the Daoist notion of natural action. Unfortunately, he did not develop his theory beyond this spare description. He may have been read in his own time, but no one of note adopted his theory, and few today have even heard of him. Why not? Because he was going against the theoretical grain of not only his time but his entire culture. In his time, the main theory of the human mind came from Descartes, who cobbled together a theory that used Christian ideas to revive Plato and Aristotle, positing a theory very much the opposite of La Mettrie's. We'll see a variety of the Cartesian view below in Rousseau, a contemporary of La Mettrie.

Jean-Jacques Rousseau

Most educated people have heard of Jean-Jacques Rousseau (1712–1778), who was an important political philosopher. Rousseau gave us the idea of the noble savage—somebody who is naturally good and not infected with the twisted conventions of society.

Like La Mettrie, Rousseau refers to human action as *spontaneous*, but he means something quite different. According to Rousseau, there is no real action without the will, by which he meant a kind of free intentionality, distinct from the rest of the human. This sounds more like Aristotle than like Laozi. The Daoists preferred an absence of intentionality, after all.

Rousseau said that matter is in motion according to fixed laws, meaning that all nonhuman, nonintentional movement is deterministic. Again, this is more Aristotelian than Daoist. Humans, however, according to Rousseau, are animated by an immaterial substance. This is the Cartesian dualism mentioned above. The immaterial substance is spirit, which is responsible for initiating movement in us. So, in addition to our material nature, we also have a spiritual nature that is the true essence of the human being.

We can see from these three features of Rousseau's theory of action (the existence of a will, determined motion in nature, and the spiritual essence of the human being) that he leans more toward Aristotle than the Daoists. However, whereas Aristotle aligned intentional action with rationality, Rousseau was mistrustful of rationality. Recall the noble savage, who relies more on instinct than on deliberating about the good and the bad. To understand Rousseau, we have to understand what he means by instinct.

For Rousseau, human instinct in its most fundamental, primitive form is divine—that is, spiritual. If we are fundamentally spiritual, and the spirit comes straight from God, it makes sense that it is perfectly good to begin with. People go astray, according to Rousseau, when they get infected with the values of civilized society. If we could bracket out the spiritual essence in his theory, Rousseau would sound more like the Daoists. But Rousseau cannot get rid of the spiritual, for that is what draws us closer to the ultimate good—God. He says:

> Man is intelligent when he reasons, and the supreme intelligence [God] does not need to reason. For it there are neither premises nor conclusions; there are not even propositions. It is purely intuitive. . . . Human power acts by means; divine power acts by itself.[20]

In order to act in the best way possible, according to Rousseau, we should aspire to act less like humans and more like God, by relying on spiritual intuition. Interestingly, Rousseau's description of action by God sounds very similar to a Daoist theory of action—there is no thinking involved; it just happens, and whatever happens is just right.

Here is the problem that Rousseau gets himself into (a problem that we Western philosophers continually get ourselves into): by saying that matter is deterministic and human beings are free, we have to resolve how human beings can be both natural and free. Rousseau does this by saying that humans, in order to have this ideal kind of action, need to be more like God. God is the ultimate model for action. God is completely free—that is, spontaneous. And for us to be spontaneous, we need to be more like God.

This is how Rousseau unifies matter and spirit in a way that looks something like *ziran* in its description of ideal action. To get to ideal action, though, notice that it requires an extra ingredient. It requires the divine. Laozi and Zhuangzi, in contrast, don't need an extra ingredient. For them, there is no separation to begin with between the free and the determined, between the spiritual (as human) and the natural (as nonhuman).[21] Because there is no separation to begin with, one doesn't need a theory about how to unify them. The natural and the human are already together.

William James

William James (1842–1910) was a psychologist and a philosopher who put a lot of thought into human psychology. In fact, his book, the *Principles of Psychology*, even though it was written more than one hundred years ago, it is still worth reading today, as it is very insightful about many aspects of human psychology, just one of which we will look at here.

James said that we can divide human movement into two basic kinds. One is *primary movement*, which involves reflexes, instinct, and emotion. This kind of movement is automatic—we don't have control over it. The second kind of movement, called *secondary movement*, refers to movement that we do have some control over.

James says there are two further components of secondary movement. The first is *ideo-motor movement*, which is habituated movement. This refers to things that we learn and can further develop over time. We have ultimate control over them but can also let them occur on their own, like walking, talking, eating, or playing the piano. The other subdivision of secondary movement is *deliberation*. This is where we find morality, freedom, and effort. James says:

> Thinking exists as a special kind of immaterial process alongside of the material processes of the world. It is certain . . . that only by postulating such thinking do we make things currently intelligible.[22]

Like Rousseau, the way that James makes sense of freedom is to move it into a nonmaterial realm. As a Pragmatist, however, he is not making a definitive claim that there is a nonmaterial realm. Rather, he is saying that given all the presuppositions we've laid out above about determinism in nature and responsibility attribution, the only way to make sense of it all is by positing an immaterial soul in humans that is the seat of free will.

By way of explaining, he says:

> The idea to be consented to must be kept from flickering
> and going out. It must be held steadily before the mind.[23]

This is his conception of attention. The idea of consent he is using here is basically a variety of the Stoic idea of assent that we saw above in Chrysippus. That was the Stoics' way of having human action be both deterministic and voluntary at the same time—an impulse arises and we either assent to it or we don't. For James, before we consent, we can also turn the idea over in our minds—that is, think about it. This is James's idea of attention. We discussed attention in a Daoist context above. Remember the cicada catcher who paid very close attention to the cicadas? James says that when this happens—when we pay attention voluntarily—it is always effortful. This is quite different from Zhuangzi's swimmer, who did it effortlessly.

When you think of what attention is, you might agree at first with James. Paying attention to these complex theories right now might feel effortful for you. Doing a math problem is also usually felt to be effortful. But think of something, such as playing a video game or playing a musical instrument, that you're very good at. You can pay close attention to these, and yet it can actually feel effortless. We will look at this issue of effortless attention in detail in the third chapter.

It is significant here that James makes this distinction because he ties effortful attention to morality. It is the effort of the will that allows us to think something through, according to James, and thereby discern the good that is to be done. In other words, James basically adopts Aristotle's view of human action and adds a little bit—the pragmatic justification and the aspect of effortfulness. As in Aristotle, we get a very strong emphasis on habit in James, which helps us appreciate this aspect of Daoist natural action, but it is still quite a bit different from Daoism because it involves a notion of free will (which is outside of nature) and effort.

Friedrich Schiller

Friedrich Schiller (1759–1805) came after Immanuel Kant (and before James) and basically adopted Kant's view of the world. Following Kant, Schiller said that there are two realms of action. One is the realm of necessity, and one is the realm of contingency.

On the necessity side (see Table 1.3), we have things that are natural and generally outside of one's control. Some examples are breathing, sensation, sympathetic action (which is basically emotionally motivated action), and then an idea that most concerns him—grace. Before discussing grace, let's compare the items on the contingency side. These are the things that a person can entirely control: singing, morality, willful action, and dignity. Although this dichotomy stems from Kant, it is not inconsistent with Aristotle's view. However, Schiller resembles Rousseau in his suspicion of human reason.

When Schiller looked at Kant's model of the good person, he didn't like what he saw. He saw somebody who is very stern, who inflexibly does the right thing, who never tells a lie. Schiller envisioned the model of the good person in quite a different way. He envisioned somebody who also is good, but somebody friendly and warm, somebody you gravitate toward instead of somebody you keep at arm's length. He says this person has grace, which is a step above dignity. What is Schiller's conception of grace? Why was it so important to him?

In the table, you see grace on the side of necessity, but this is what he says about it: it is "beauty of movement that is outside of nature in the realm of freedom." In the sense that it is free, it should properly be placed on the contingency side of the table. Freedom, for Schiller, however, has an artificial tinge to it. Graceful action is beautiful, and beauty belongs to nature. In other words, Schiller sees the fundamental problem in human action that we have discussed—namely, that the most beautiful (and good) kind of action must be natural (echoing Rousseau's ideal of the noble savage), and yet free action must be artificial

Table 1.3. Schiller's Necessity and Contingency Dichotomy

NECESSITY (NATURAL) OUTSIDE OF ONE'S CONTROL	CONTINGENCY (VOLUNTARY) UNDER ONE'S CONTROL
Breathing	Singing
Sensation	Morality
Sympathetic (emotional) action	Willful action
Grace	Dignity

(echoing Aristotle's ideal of deliberative rationality). How does Schiller reconcile these two? This is what he says:

> When a monarchic state is run in such a way that, although everything proceeds in accordance with the will of one person, the individual citizen can still persuade himself that he is living according to his own lights and simply following his inclinations, one calls this a liberal government. However, one would be very hesitant to give it this name if either the ruler imposed his will against the citizen's inclinations or the citizen imposed his inclinations against the will of the ruler.[24]

This should sound familiar. It sounds just like Laozi. And it also sounds just like what Aristotle said about the movement of animals through his metaphor of the "well-governed commonwealth." The king is in charge of the government, but the king doesn't have to do anything—*wu wei*—everything just happens. To Schiller, this is a metaphor for grace, for how a graceful person acts. The graceful person doesn't have to think about each movement—it just happens, and yet it is just right. It is the most rational thing to do, as if it had been deliberated ahead of time.

Now consider another passage from Schiller:

> The general feeling alone among humans makes ease into the main characteristic of grace, and where effort is required, ease can never be the outcome. It is also clear that, on the other hand, nature ought never to use force against the mind if a beautiful, moral expression is to occur, for wherever nature reigns alone, humanity disappears.[25]

There is no difference between what Schiller's graceful person does and what the Kantian dignified person would do, but what the graceful person does comes off as beautiful and natural. This is ideal action for Schiller.

It looks as if Schiller has successfully unified freedom and determinism in the concept of grace, that he has solved the problem that plagued Western philosophy for two thousand years. And it looks a lot like Daoist natural action. However, as with Rousseau, to really pull this off requires an extra ingredient. Here is what Schiller says:

> Love . . . flows forth from the seat of freedom, from our divine nature. . . . It is absolute greatness itself . . . the legislator himself, the God in us, who plays with his own image in the world of senses.[26]

Thus, the way that Schiller in the end unifies the human and the natural is through God. The only way for us to be graceful is to appeal to the spiritual in us. This is not metaphorical. This is actual. He believes that there is a spirit inside us. Just as with Rousseau, the conscience is the divine instinct. Given the starting assumptions of determinism and responsibility ascription in the West, resorting to the concept of God seems to be the only way to unify the natural and the human.

Conclusion

Now we have seen several examples of something like *ziran* in the West. Because of the divide between the concepts of freedom and determinism, however, it is monumentally difficult to unify the human and the natural without some kind of divine intervention, an appeal to something that is nonmaterial, nonphysical, nonnatural.

Here is a question for us today. As philosophers, we don't just describe theories, we evaluate them. So, which is true? Who is right? If we are thoroughly scientific about it, if we follow Darwin, for example, we have to say that human beings are natural—fundamentally natural. Therefore, we cannot appeal to a spiritual essence. We cannot appeal to an immaterial source of action or goodness. This perspective of naturalism is also consistent with Laozi and Zhuangzi.

In their naturalistic assumptions, Laozi and Zhuangzi[27] seem more contemporary than some of our most famous Western philosophers—Aristotle, Rousseau, Schiller, even the scientist William James. So maybe these Daoists have something to teach us. Maybe we can take a key idea of theirs and use it to solve some contemporary problems that we are unable to solve because we have been indoctrinated with Western ideas about human action. These Western ideas persist today in our sciences, even though we try to be as objective as possible. These assumptions are baked in to how we see the world, and they get taught and handed down from generation to generation.

As an alternative, if we can use a perspective from early China that is consistent with the overall way that we think that the world should work—naturalistically—then maybe it can help solve some of our persistent problems. This is what we shall do in the following chapters. We shall apply this Daoist idea of natural action to contemporary philosophy of action, to cognitive science, and to aesthetics.

Chapter 2

Saving Natural Human Action from the Paradox of Spontaneity

In what follows, I shall present a fairly complex argument, mostly about Western philosophy. I'll try to keep the ideas as straightforward as possible and explain them as clearly and briefly as possible, beginning with the basic idea of the philosophy of action. Philosophy of action as a field would be mystifying to an ancient Chinese thinker, who would not have begun with a free will/determinism dichotomy, as occurs in the dominant Western tradition (see below).

Let's start with this question: How is what humans do distinct from what sunflowers do when both are in motion? Imagine there is a sunflower. In the morning when the sun comes up in the east, the sunflower faces the sun. As the sun moves across the sky, the sunflower tracks it. Even though sunflowers are just plants, they move, of course. Philosophers who do philosophy of action inquire into the fundamental nature of movement, with questions such as: What is the difference between what the sunflower is doing when it is moving and what we are doing when we are moving? This can seem like an uninteresting question until you complicate it a bit. Now suppose I am sitting in front of the sunflower, and as the sunflower is tracking the sun, I am tracking the sunflower. Both the sunflower and I are moving at the same pace, more or less in the same way. I have a nervous system, so that's different. But that is not what is interesting to the philosopher of action.

Suppose further that there is a power line next to the sunflower. As the sunflower is moving, it bumps into the electrical wire and starts a fire. Could we blame the sunflower? "You bad sunflower. How dare you be so careless?!" That does not make a lot of sense. On the other hand, if the power line is near me, and as I am tracking the sunflower,

I bump into the power line and start a fire, knowing full well that it is there and what could happen, I could be blamed. This is the issue that a philosopher of action is trying to answer: Why should I be blamed? What is it about my motion that we can ascribe responsibility to it? In the field of the philosophy of action, responsibility ascription is a mark of *action*. We can ask the narrow question more broadly: What makes human action distinct from other forms of motion in nature? Responsibility is one way that philosophers in the West have tried to distinguish action specifically from motion more generally. This question will become clearer as we go. It is one of the underlying questions of everything to be discussed in this chapter.

I want you to notice one particular thing about this subject matter. We have to distinguish two different terms. The first is *action*, which is reserved for the possibility of responsibility ascription. Everything else is described by some more vague term, such as *motion, movement,* or *behavior*. Action, therefore, is a kind of motion, but motion isn't necessarily action. That is why this field is called philosophy of action. The term *action* is a technical term. Notice also that this distinction drives a wedge between nature on one hand and humans on the other. Suddenly, there's a gap between the two. This is something that has troubled Western philosophy for centuries. In chapter 1, we discussed *ziran* and saw in the Chinese tradition no such distinction and, therefore, no such problem. In this chapter, we will discuss how to bring over the Chinese idea of *ziran* to help bridge this gap between the human and the natural in the West.

Recall from chapter 1 the idea of *ziran*, an idea unique to China. *Ziran* is a word for motion that originates internally, is absent external interference, and involves multivalent causality. The motion of *ziran* is absent overt intentionality. The psychology of *ziran* involves high concentration and freedom from distraction. It is efficient in that it is accurately responsive to subtle cues. Finally, it is marked by a feeling of ease. What is notable about the concept of *ziran* for us right now is that there is no division between the natural and the human. In fact, the natural is considered an ideal model of human behavior.

In chapter 1, we also looked at several philosophers in the West seeking equivalent ideas to *ziran*. One of the main philosophers we looked at was Aristotle, who had four candidates for possible equivalents of *ziran*. After considering all four, we summarized the differences between *ziran* motion and Aristotle's notion of action, reproduced here as Table 2.1.

Notice from the table that in Daoism, nature is the ideal model of action, whereas for Aristotle, nature represents unrestrained action. If you are acting naturally, Aristotle would say that you are not there yet—you have not achieved ideal action. In Daoism, deliberation can be debilitating. We saw, for example, the story of the swimmer who was in roiling water. If he stopped to think about what he should do next, he'd be sucked under the water and drown. For Aristotle, deliberation is a necessary step to the good. In Daoism, ideal action (*ziran*, translated in the table as *spontaneity*), is conceived as achieving optimal results, whereas for Aristotle, it is conceived as achieving the ethical good. In Daoism, spontaneity is the highest form of action, whereas for Aristotle, spontaneity is a lower form of action. It is something that kids and animals do. This comparison gives us a little bit of a hint of where we will be going in this chapter and lays a nice groundwork for what follows.

In chapter 1, we also discussed something I called the paradox of spontaneity. In the process of looking for equivalent notions of *ziran* in the West, the term *spontaneity* kept arising as a potential equivalent of *ziran* in the West. This term appears in French as *spontaneité* and in German as *spontaneität*, both of which originate from the Latin *sponte*. Strangely, though, when the term is used—in whatever European language—it is used in two mutually contradictory ways. The basic idea is *movement achieved without external interference*. When

Table 2.1. *Ziran* vs. Aristotelian action

DAOIST SPONTANEITY	ARISTOTLE'S ACTION
Nature as the ideal model of action	Nature represents unrestrained action
Deliberation is debilitating	Deliberation leads to the good
Action conceived as achieving optimal results	Action conceived as achieving the ethical good
Spontaneity is the highest form of action	Spontaneity is a lower form of action

this is applied to nature, it means that the motion is determined by natural forces. For example, we could use this sense to say that grass grows spontaneously. There's nobody out there pulling at the grass or otherwise trying to make it grow. It grows of its own accord, as natural. When the word is applied to humans, however, it refers to motion that is *not* determined by natural forces, but from human free will. I call this a paradox because motion is called spontaneous in that it is part of nature and spontaneous in that it is separate from nature, and it cannot be both.

In technical philosophical terminology, we have a paradox (more specifically, an antinomy) when two statements both appear to be true and yet cannot both be true.

1. Motion is spontaneous in that it is part of nature.

2. Motion is spontaneous in that it is separate from nature.

I call this the paradox of spontaneity. In this chapter, I'll show how we can resolve this paradox and one related paradox.

Here is a basic outline of this chapter:

Part 1: Natural human action as theoretically impossible

Part 2: Self-organization as a model for all motion

Part 3: Two kinds of motive self

Part 4: Three candidates for natural human action

Conclusion: Natural human action is possible, even desirable

Natural Human Action Is Theoretically Impossible

Recall that the main theme of this book is that there are ideas from early Chinese philosophy that can profit the world, even in cutting edge fields. In this chapter, I build on the idea of *ziran* to show how it can be put to use in contemporary philosophy of action, one of the core fields of contemporary Analytic philosophy. In contemporary philosophy, natural human action is theoretically impossible. By "theoretically impossible," I don't mean that it could be practically possible but is impossible only in theory. According to philosophers, when something is theoretically impossible, it cannot be possible at all because there would be a contradiction involved, and contradictions are not allowed. In what follows, I will expose this contradiction along two avenues. One is through aesthetics, and the other is through the philosophy of action.

Any philosopher who might be reading this might already be thinking that by discussing a topic of philosophy of action by way of the field of aesthetics I'll be making a category mistake. "Why discuss aesthetics in a chapter about the philosophy of action?" I do this because it can help us understand the problem better; also because I'll be returning to aesthetics later on in the book. I am generally skeptical of the complaint of the category mistake. It is a common way of quickly dismissing an argument in philosophy. Sometimes the accusation is legitimate, but too often it prevents analysis from a distinct, useful perspective. Sometimes our linguistic or conceptual categories push us in directions that get us into philosophical difficulties. Looking at an issue via different categories can help us confront gaps that sometimes we are content to gloss over.

In the field of aesthetics, which deals with the theory of beauty and art, philosophers have noticed something interesting about how we approach art. We approach it differently from how we approach, say, a common drinking cup. When we think of a drinking cup (if we think of one at all), we tend to think of what it can do for us practically. But then maybe we come across a lovely ceramic tea cup, which we appreciate it for its beauty instead of just for its practicality.

There are questions we can ask about art that help us understand it more, and by understanding it more, we can appreciate it more—aesthetically. As an example, consider a simple aesthetic pursuit such as drinking tea or wine. People often say that the more you know about wine, the more you appreciate it. Tea aficionados say the same about tea. The same goes for fine art, such as painting and symphonic music. Consider the Mona Lisa. We ask questions about it such as:

What medium did the artist use?

What is the theme?

Who is the artist?

What does some feature (the smile) mean?

How does is this work fit into the period?

How does it fit into the artist's oeuvre?

What did the work mean to people of the artist's time?

What is the deeper meaning?

Exploring the answers to these questions helps us appreciate a work of art aesthetically. Recently, philosophers have been thinking not just about how we appreciate art and artifacts but also how we aesthetically appreciate nature. I'm sure you have walked through a garden, looked at the flowers, and appreciated their beauty. However, none of the questions above are available in helping us deepen our appreciation of a rosebud or an old-growth forest. Philosophers who do aesthetics are puzzled by this. How can we have what seems to be the same kind of aesthetic experience but with a very different intellectual foundation?

Some philosophers have put a lot of thought into the differences between appreciating art aesthetically and appreciating nature aesthetically. Here are three relevant quotations from academic articles on the subject:

- The aesthetic appreciation of nature . . . is identical with the aesthetic appreciation not of that which is nature, but of nature *as nature and not as art (or artifact).*[1]

- Natural objects . . . lack a human maker.[2]

- Aesthetic experience of nature always demands our realizing that nature itself is a nonartistic object, not designed by any artist for our admiration, not framed or put on a pedestal—all this is much of the secret of nature's aesthetic power, construct though we may the aesthetic categories through which such nature is experienced.[3]

Reading these quotations carefully, we see that humans, and human artifacts, are excluded from being objects of aesthetic appreciation in terms of being natural. That is, when we appreciate nature, we appreciate it in that it is not human. What does that imply for the aesthetic appreciation of motion? It implies that the aesthetic appreciation of natural motion precludes human action as natural in the realm of art. It makes *natural human action* theoretically impossible. Why? Because if appreciation of nature excludes humans, it would be impossible to appreciate human action as natural. I am here taking the word *natural* literally, not as just a metaphor.

I don't know about you, but I find this conclusion about the impossibility of natural human action difficult to accept because when I look at some human action, such as dance, I feel as though I should be able to characterize it as natural, and not just metaphorically. Intuitively, it seems problematic to say that human action cannot be natural.

This conclusion about humans necessarily being outside of nature comes from the field of aesthetics and gives us an avenue that makes the problem I am addressing easy to understand. We'll return to aesthetics later. For now, let us turn back to philosophy of action proper.

In Ancient Greece, where much of Western philosophy has its roots, there is the notion that all events are fated. For example, you may have heard of the story of Oedipus. When Oedipus was born, a soothsayer predicted that he would grow up to kill his father and marry his mother. To prevent that, his parents tried to kill him. They had him set out on a hillside, where he was expected to die. Instead, he was saved and grew up. And lo and behold, he eventually, and unknowingly, murdered his father and married his mother. The moral of the story is that no matter how hard you try, you cannot escape fate. This idea of ineluctable fate had a companion in metaphysical determinism, which evolved with it over the history of Western philosophy. When our scientific theories started to flourish in the Enlightenment, the idea transformed decisively from fatalism to determinism—the view that the laws of nature are inescapable. As science became more and more exact, it was as if there was no flexibility in the laws of nature at all. If one thing is on course to collide with another, absent any kind of interference, it will inevitably happen. Insofar as everything is subject to the laws of nature, then everything is determined.[4]

According to this view, if we can know exactly where everything is, the direction it is moving, the force that is pushing it, etc., then we can predict exactly what will happen in the future.

The view of fatalism/determinism is problematic, especially for somebody such as Aristotle who wanted to be able to ascribe responsibility to people for their actions. According to a deterministic view, if I go and cut off somebody's finger, while at the same time being entirely subject to the laws of nature, you cannot blame me. You can only blame the forces of nature acting on me. It's not my fault. The basic problem in philosophy of action is trying to figure out how in a world that's naturally determined we can also ascribe responsibility.

Notice this gap between the human and nature. Only humans can be ascribed responsibility. Nature came to be characterized as having only determined motion, and human beings came to be viewed as outside of that. As a result, human action must be distinct from natural motion, making *natural* human action impossible. I believe this is a significant problem. And it is a consequence of the Western tradition of philosophy of action. Maybe it can be repaired. But let's be clear first why it is a paradox.

It is a paradox because although our theory tells us that it's true that natural human action is impossible, we also know that we are fundamentally natural beings. Here, again, we have two propositions that appear to be true but cannot both be true. We know that we're natural because we are part of a phylogenetic unity. We all have DNA that evolved out of other kinds of creatures all the way back to blue-green algae, some distant time in the past. We cannot deny that we are natural creatures in that sense. We also actually use the term *natural,* in a literal way—not a metaphorical way—when we say things such as, "Breastfeeding is natural." For the infant, it is clearly *natural* behavior. For the modern mother, who chooses to breastfeed her baby, it is natural *action* in the technical sense of having chosen to do it and being able to ascribe responsibility.

We can say, then, that breastfeeding is a counterexample to the proposition that natural human action is impossible. Unfortunately, that doesn't settle anything. However, it can motivate the idea that natural human action is part of our normal way of viewing the world. Similarly, art is not something that's fundamentally separated from nature. There are now quite a few scholarly books laying out theories of why the production of art is evolutionarily adaptive. On this view, art was an extension of tool making, an evolved behavior making us better able to survive and flourish. In this sense, art is fundamentally natural.

There is another reason to doubt the claim that natural human action is impossible. It is that despite the long history of philosophy of action in the West, there really is no convincing account of metaphysical freedom. How could it be that everything in the world is subject to natural law except human beings? How are we somehow divorced from nature? Advocates of free will say that we are separate from nature, outside of natural laws, when we choose freely to act. But how could that even be possible? What is the mechanism? What is the causal chain? Nobody has been able to say. There is no convincing metaphysical account of this kind of freedom.[5]

I hope you see the paradox now: natural human action is impossible, but it cannot be impossible. Let's see if we can resolve the paradox. I'm going to introduce the notion of *self-organization*. And I'm going to say that it will account for natural behavior in humans and it will account for artifice in nature. In other words, it will close the gap between humans and nature. I will begin with the second part—artifice in nature—because it helps motivate the first part and makes it more understandable.

There is a bird in New Guinea called the bowerbird. The evolutionary biologist Gerald Borgia says this about the bowerbird:

> The male satin bowerbird's bower consists of two parallel walls made of fine twigs that stand on a court cleared on the ground. The walls are 10cm apart and form a 30-cm central avenue. Males decorate a stick platform on the north end of their bowers with a variety of objects including feathers, flowers, and snake skins. Bowers are used as sites for courting females, and mating takes place inside the bower; males steal decorations and destroy the bowers of other males.[6]

The behavior of this variety of bowerbird is often depicted as involving aesthetic choices in how it displays the objects around the bower, which vary widely. Is it possible that there could be action (in the technical philosophical sense) or artifice, in nature? The example of the bowerbird seems to suggest that both might be possible. In this sense, the bowerbird complicates our picture. One way to close the nature-human gap is by finding human action that is natural, such as breastfeeding. In the bowerbird, we might close the gap by finding genuine action, or artifice, in the nonhuman realm.

Let's look at this more closely. The bowerbird builds a bower. It is not a house. The bower has one function only—as a display to attract a mate. It is sort of like a teenage boy's muscle car that he uses to attract girls. What is the difference between what the bowerbird does and what a sixteen-year-old boy does? Or consider a three-year-old making sand castles at the beach. The sand castles are examples of artifice but not artifice in the same way as with a full-blown artist.

When philosophers discuss freedom, determinism, action, and art, they generally begin with the case of the competent adult and discuss borderline cases only to make particular points. I think it helps to begin with borderline cases because it helps complicate the matter and show that our initial assumptions are not as tidy as they are often made out to be.

The bowerbird and the child making sand castles are boundary cases in the question of artifice in nature. We can ask if their behavior counts as (1) artifice and (2) natural. Robert Aunger is an anthropologist. He defines *artifice* in the following way:

> The enduring forms or structures created by animals through niche constructive behaviour primarily to be used in a way that increases their biological fitness.[7]

Notice that he says "animals" (which does not exclude humans) and that he characterizes the process as fundamentally biological. That's another way of saying *natural*. To this scientist, then, there is indeed such a thing as artifice in nature. The bowerbird would definitely be an example, as would the child building sandcastles and the teenage boy fixing up his muscle car.

Now we have opened our assumptions about nature, action, and artifice to examination and see that the human-nature gap in Western philosophy of action is challenging but not unbridgeable.

Self-Organization as a Model for All Motion

Self-organization is an idea that you rarely see in philosophy generally, let alone the philosophy of action specifically. But you do see it in the sciences. In what follows, I will attempt to import it from the sciences into philosophy of action. I want to emphasize that I am not using a marginal idea that scientists rarely use. This is now a fundamental idea in the sciences and is used quite often. For example, I did a search just recently in a database of science (the Web of Science) that brought up more than twenty thousand peer reviewed articles that use this term specifically. And this is not the only term that can refer to the general concept. There are also terms such as *complex systems theory, dynamic systems theory,* and you may have heard of *chaos theory*. All of these refer to an idea that began in physics and has spread to biology and to the social sciences and now, hopefully, can also be spread to philosophy.

I also did a search in the Philosophers Index for this idea and found that there are fewer than ten philosophy articles that use the term *self-organization* (or related term) and that are relevant to the philosophy of action. It is encouraging that there are some such articles out there, but there is still a long way to go in fully implementing the idea. (In the philosophy of science, you can find a few more examples.)

In trying to understand the concept of self-organization, let's begin with a more familiar idea—the idea of *entropy*. I'm sure you were introduced to the idea of entropy in high school Physics class. Entropy is the idea that everything tends toward disorder. This is the second law of thermodynamics. For example, eventually all stars will burn out. You clean up your room, but it gets messy again. Self-organization is the opposite of entropy. In fact, people have wondered if self-organization is a violation of the second law of thermodynamics. I think it is now agreed that it is not a violation. If it were a violation of a natural law, that would be odd, because self-organization also seems to be a natural law of sorts, and we see it virtually everywhere.

Self-organization is when things in nature collect together and form what can be called a *self*. Hence the term *self-organization*. You see it in clouds, in cells, in leaves, in gusts of wind, in animals. And not just in the animal but in populations of animals. When populations form, they also can be understood as self-organized entities. Almost anywhere in nonhuman nature that you see organization is an example of self-organization. This idea is out there all around us all the time, but we rarely think about it, and scientists are just now trying to take full account of it, including social scientists and, hopefully, philosophers as well.

What are the philosophical implications of this idea from physics? What if we take this idea and we say, "Let's start here and see if we can understand human motion as an example of self-organization"? After all, self-organization is natural. Approaching human action in this way might give us an avenue to say that human action can also be natural. This approach is distinct from the usual approach of assuming that all natural motion is strictly determined and then being unable to apply it to "freely" chosen human behavior. I am not saying that self-organization is not deterministic. That's a subject for a different day. What I am saying is that we can set the deterministic assumption aside (since it is far from being definitively established) and use a different principle of natural motion to approach the topic of human behavior.

Two Kinds of Motive Self

In this section, I shall describe two kinds of self, and one of them will rely on the idea of self-organization. Let's start with the first kind of self, but let's go back a step farther. Before we talk about an actual self, let's look at the use of the prefix *self-*. Our language represents the concepts we use to understand the world. And sometimes our language, via these concepts, picks out real things in the world—assuming that our language has the capacity to describe reality, and assuming that there is one objective reality. Therefore, it is possible that by examining our language, we can get a purchase on our metaphysics.[8] Let's look first at our language. How do we use the hyphenated *self*?

Here are some examples:

Self-enrichment

Self-doubt

Self-immolation

A person reading this book may be doing so for the purpose of self-enrichment. As such, you would be enriching your *self*. Notice that when we use the term *self-enrichment*, there is a single subject (a), who is performing an action (verb) on an object (b). Under this construal, the sentence can be formalized as:

$$\text{Verb}(a,b)$$

Now notice that a and b are identical—they are both the self. So we should revise the formula:

$$\text{Verb}(a,a)$$

As far as the verb goes, in this usage, the hyphenated *self* implies a voluntary impetus stemming from the single entity a, and affecting itself, a.

What about self-doubt? If you are unfamiliar with the field of philosophy, you may have felt some self-doubt in picking up this book, thinking, "Will I be able to understand it?" In the usage of the term *self-doubt,* we again see the formula:

$$\text{Verb}(a,a)$$

When I was originally writing up these ideas, I read in the news about self-immolation. This is when somebody sets oneself on fire. Again, the formula is:

$$\text{Verb}(a,a)$$

This formula—this way of speaking—says something about how we think of a person acting. There is an individual entity with an internal impetus that originates from the individual entity and is directed back at that individual entity.

There is another way that we use the prefix *self-* in English. Consider the following terms:

Self-government

Self-fertilization

Self-organization

Consider, first, self-government. A democracy is an example of self-government. In this use of the hyphenated *self,* instead of an individual entity acting on the same individual, we have a whole group of individuals acting in various ways that add up to cooperation. There is still an identifiable self, but instead of a discrete entity, it is a group of interrelated entities. Instead of an internal impetus stemming from one entity, we see plural interaction—individuals (or parts) acting together for a purpose that aids the larger self. Person a votes, person b speaks up, person c demonstrates, person d holds office, and so on. It is difficult to write a formula for this kind of "self-" action, but it might look something like this:

$$Verb_1 Verb_2 Verb_3 Verb_4 Verb_5(abcde,[abcde])$$

The square brackets indicate that there is a unified self toward the goals of which the individual parts are actively working. We might be tempted to write the formula like this:

$$Verb_1 Verb_2 Verb_3 Verb_4 Verb_5([abcde],[abcde])$$

with the square brackets indicating an individual entity—the self—doing the actions. But such a formulation suggests that the whole entity is performing each of the actions $Verb_1$, $Verb_2$, $Verb_3$, and so on. That would be incorrect because what makes it self-organization is the very plurality of it—each part acting individually and yet in concert with the other parts. It is difficult to put this into standard logical notation because our logical notation was created for discrete individual entities (the first kind of "self-"), not for individuals as interrelated parts plurally interacting (the second kind of "self-").

In the case of self-fertilization, we see a simplified version of this complex process. In self-fertilization of, say, a plant, we see just two related parts. One part releases the pollen, and one part is receptive to it. The formalization would be something like this:

$$Verb_1 Verb_2(ab,c,[abcde])$$

The individual acts are $Verb_1(a,c)$ (the pollen (c) is released by one part of the plant (a)) and $Verb_2(b,c)$ (the pollen is caught by another part (b)), all toward one of the implicit goals of the whole plant—[abcde][9]—perpetuation of the species.

Both self-governance and self-fertilization are examples of self-organization, examples of plural interaction in which different parts of a self interact to further the interests of the larger self. What the two kinds of "self-" motion have in common is the internal impetus. Where they differ is in (1) the origin of the impetus (single versus plural) and (2) the object (also single versus plural—but plural in a way that it is also single at a higher level).

These two sets of examples of the use of *self-* show how our language can help us understand our world. Through further observation, we can easily conclude that there is a single kind of self that is structurally simple, and there is a plural kind of self that is structurally complex (see Table 2.2). The impetus of both of them is internal (that is why we use the word *spontaneous* for both of them, although it does give rise to the paradox of spontaneity already discussed—more about this later). The impetus of the motion of the single self is singly sourced, meaning that the motivation, the impulse to act, is traceable to just one single entity—to me, to the individual subject. The plural self, by contrast, is multiply sourced, meaning that the impetus of actions arises from many distinct individuals that somehow function cooperatively. The single self is directive—sending out a kind of command: "Do this." The plural self is interactive—different actions combining to produce a purposeful-like effect.

This distinction between the single self and the plural self is, I am suggesting, a feature of our world discoverable through the way that we use our language to describe the world and through introspection. There are single selves out there, and there are plural selves out there.[10]

In philosophy, when we talk about selves we often wonder about ourselves in terms of personal identity. What is it that makes me the same person as the little baby who was crawling around in 1967? My parents called that baby Brian, and I'm also called Brian today. But these two people are very different. That little baby couldn't discuss philosophy, and I can't suck on my toes. What philosophers have said is that one of the key ideas of identity over time is the notion of phenomenality, or consciousness—the fact that I can think and feel and that I think and feel like the same person over time. It's the same *me* in terms of awareness.

Table 2.2. Single and Plural Self

SINGLE SELF	PLURAL SELF
Structurally simple	Structurally complex
Impetus is:	Impetus is:
• Internal	• Internal
• Singly sourced	• Multiply sourced
• Directive	• Interactive

There are many ways that philosophers discuss self-identity, and this is just one way, a way that I want to use to introduce a concept that can help us understand and discuss these two kinds of self. It will move us from the realm of just motion into the realm of action.

To discuss the single self, I want now to introduce the term *Φ-self*, meaning *phenomenal self*. Φ (pronounced *fie*) is a Greek letter. It is equivalent to *ph* in English. Philosophers have a special affection for this letter (because "philosophy" starts with "ph") and use Φ often as an abbreviation. "Phenomenal" also starts with *ph*, so using the Greek letter Φ is a convenient abbreviation for referring to this single kind of self. The Φ-self is a self that I define as having a phenomenal sense, meaning that the self is aware of the self and aware of the world. A *C-self*, I suggest, is a complex, meaning a group of things functioning together for unified purposes. It is a self-organizing complex. Since "complex" begins with the letter *c*, I call it a C-self. A Φ-self has a phenomenal sense of self. A C-self is a self-organizing complex.

A Φ-self is human, or maybe a bowerbird, or a chimpanzee, or some other animal that is conscious, or self-aware. A C-self is any self-organized system (see Table 2.3). So a C-self could be a human, a system of organs in the human body, a cell in the human body, a cell inside a worm, a cloud, a tree—any self-organizing complex at any level of complexity.

An interesting thing about the Φ-self is that it goes away and then comes back again. When I go to sleep at night, my Φ-self vanishes. It's not there anymore. And when I wake up in the morning, there it is again. When I take a nap in the afternoon, it goes away. When I wake up, it comes back. I'm conscious, then I'm unconscious, then I'm conscious again. The C-self, in contrast, doesn't do that. It is persistent.

Table 2.3. Two Kinds of Self

Φ-SELF	C-SELF
Phenomenal sense of self	Self-organizing complex
Human/animal	Any self-organized system, including humans
Intermittent	Persistent
Rooted in the C-self	May give rise to a Φ-self

When it goes away, it goes away for good. Once it stops self-organizing, the various parts are subject to entropy. When a cell dies, it doesn't come back. When humans die, we don't come back.

A Φ-self is rooted in a C-self. You cannot have a Φ-self without a C-self. A C-self may give rise to aw-self or it may not.

With these definitions in place, we can get to the possibility of natural human action. Because the C-self, as a self-organizing complex, is fundamentally natural, any motion stemming from it is natural motion. And so we now have a practical way of stipulating a definition of natural behavior. *Natural* behavior is self-organized, meaning that:

1. The motive impulse is internal.
2. The motive impulse is plural.

From this definition, we can immediately conclude that Φ-self behavior, because it does not meet criterion #2, cannot be classified as natural behavior.

Notice what we've done here. We've taken the classic Western human/nature dichotomy and reconstrued it. Instead of a human/nature dichotomy, which would preclude natural human action, we have a Φ-self/C-self dichotomy. Only C-self behavior can be natural, but because human behavior can be classified as either Φ-self behavior or as C-self behavior, the possibility of natural human action is not precluded from the start. All we have to do is identify a kind of human behavior as C-self behavior to find natural human behavior. Going a step farther, if it also qualifies as action in the technical sense, then we have found a case of natural human action.

Artifice is the word we'll use for the opposite of natural behavior. Artifice stems from a Φ-self. This gives us the following two definitions:

Artifice—Any behavior stemming from a Φ-self and felt to be directed by a monadic internal impetus.

Natural behavior—Any behavior stemming from a self-organized system, by dint of that self-organization.

Now we can stop and think of whether it is possible for your Φ-self to go away such that the only way to account for your subsequent behavior is in terms of your C-self. We have already said that the Φ-self is intermittent. When it does go away, is it possible for there to be human behavior? If so, is it also possible that that behavior can be classified, in the technical, philosophical sense, as genuine action? If both of these criteria can be met—which doesn't seem obviously possible at the moment—then we will have found an example of natural human action.

Superior Performance of the Divided Self

One way to help us think about the technical aspect of action is through the usual way that philosophers classify motion as action. Philosophers use a set of criteria something like the following:

$$\text{phenomenal self} \leftrightarrow \text{volition} \leftrightarrow \text{action}$$

The double arrow is a logical operator, meaning that two things necessarily entail each other. Without one, you cannot have the other. In this construction, we have a so-called agent—the person performing the action—but instead of using the broad term *agent*, we can pare it down to the most essential part of the agent, namely, the phenomenal self. Without a phenomenal self, according to the traditional formulation, there is no agency.

In between the phenomenal self and the action, there has to be volition, or something like it. Philosophers have referred to this mental activity as volition, intention, guidance, or some such, and there has been much debate about what to call it and how to define it. For our purposes here, we don't need to narrow down its actual meaning, and we can randomly select any of the usual candidates. "Volition" will work fine.

This formula with the double arrows shows us the typical way of thinking of action in the West. Action requires a phenomenal agent performing a mental act,[11] which results in an outward motion. For there to be action, all three have to be present. Without volition, there can be no action. Without phenomenal agency, there can be no volition and so no action. We can discuss it in a positive sense as well. If there is action, that implies volition, which implies phenomenality.

I think this way of thinking about action is misguided, and I'll demonstrate why. It gives us a typical metaphysical approach to defining action. The phenomenal self—the agent—is usually construed as some kind of metaphysical entity. That entity initiates the mental act, which eventuates in action. When we originally discussed the notion of action in Western philosophy above, specifically with reference to Aristotle, we discussed it in terms of responsibility ascription, not metaphysical agency. What Western philosophers tend to do is to elide these two—responsibility ascription and metaphysical agency. What we'll see below is that these two can be, and should be, separated. We'll see that metaphysical agency is an unnecessary concept, and we can rely instead on simple responsibility ascription as a criterion for action.

What we'll do now is entertain three cases of behavior from contemporary experimental psychology to see if we can classify any of them as natural human action. Following our two criteria above, they must be (1) C-self behavior (the Φ-self must not be involved in causing the behavior) and (2) ascribable to that particular C-self (and not to the Φ-self) in terms of responsibility.

The first thing we need to do is realize that although the Φ-self is subjectively experienced as a monad—as a single, indivisible entity—it is actually not a monad. It is a unity. There are many aspects to our mental life that come together to give us a sense of phenomenal experience: thoughts, feelings, desires, memories, hopes, skills, and so on. Suppose you are engaged in an action, and the key part of that action involves one of these aspects of your mental life. Now suppose that this one mental aspect suddenly goes offline. It is not available. Can we still call the resultant movement an action? Will you even be able to execute the behavior? If the answer is yes to both of these, can we still say that the Φ-self is responsible for executing the action, or will we be forced to ascribe it to the remainder—to the C-self?

If an action is performed by a person, and the Φ-self is not responsible, then the only thing left is the C-self. If it is genuine action and the C-self is responsible, then we have found a case—following our definition above—of natural human action. As we consider the following three cases, keep in mind that we are looking for two specific criteria. First, the Φ-self has to be diminished to the point that we cannot ascribe responsibility to it. Second, there has to be an identifiable action (in the technical sense), not just behavior.

Our first candidate for non-Φ-self behavior that can be classified as action is sleepwalking—not just sleep*walking* but sleep behavior more broadly. Sleepwalking is a real phenomenon and refers to people who get up and do things while still technically asleep. For example, one of my students told me about a roommate of his who would get up at night while still asleep, and if people were sitting in the living room talking, he would go out and sit with them and have a whole conversation, which he would not remember in the morning. According to this student, the others knew that this other person wasn't really with it, but he could still carry on a conversation of sorts. Scientists have documented a wide variety of sleepwalking behavior, including, in addition to walking and talking, fighting, cooking, and sex. In fact, there are several legal cases of what is called the sleepwalking defense. People accused of murder have been exonerated based on this defense.

Notice the relevance of such a defense to our topic here. A person commits murder but claims to not be responsible because he was asleep the whole time. In other words, the person is saying that the Φ-self was not present, and because the Φ-self was not present, the person could not be responsible. This case meets the first criterion for natural human action above—there is behavior that is attributable to the C-self (and not the Φ-self). According to the defense, however, it would not meet the second criterion because responsibility cannot be ascribed to the person.

Sleepwalking is an interesting example because it gives us behavior in which the Φ-self clearly goes away. At the very least, it shows us that C-self behavior in humans is possible. We might continue to debate whether any sleepwalking behavior meets the criterion of responsibility ascription, but any such claim would be difficult to establish definitively. Instead of doing that, let's move to two more cases, where, I will claim, we can get a more definitive answer.

Hypnosis is also a real thing. You've probably seen in the movies where somebody swings a watch on a chain and another person's eyes glaze over because they've fallen into a trance. The person doing the hypnosis can make a suggestion, such as, "When you wake up and you hear me snap my fingers, you will bark like a dog." When the person comes out of the trance, and the hypnotist snaps her fingers, the person inexplicably starts barking like a dog—apparently through no volition of her own. The hypnotist can hypnotize the person again and wipe out the suggestion.

Under hypnosis, many features normally identified with the Φ-self, such as memories, habits, desires, and so on, can be disassociated and no longer identified with the person as part of the person's normal, cognitive-affective repertoire. This is why psychotherapists can sometimes use it to treat such things as addiction, PTSD, and chronic pain. Interestingly, the reverse can happen as well. Features not normally associated with a person can be incorporated.

Consider the following possibility. There is some kind of activity that requires one of several parts of your normal mental repertoire. Under hypnosis, that part is temporarily erased from your awareness. Nevertheless, you can still do the activity, or even do it better. If this happens and you feel as if you're doing the activity, then it must be the C-self that is doing it. If the C-self is doing it well, maybe it rises to the level of action, in the technical sense of responsibility ascription.

Responsibility is a difficult thing to pin down. We typically think of it in terms of blame, of who committed a wrong. We can also think of it, however, in terms of praise, of who performed an action that is praiseworthy. This sense of responsibility ascription will be relevant going forward.

Now, instead of discussing hypothetical possibilities, let's turn to an actual case from science. In the cognitive scientific study of attention, there is a test that reveals something very interesting about human cognition. The test is called the Stroop task. Before we jump to the Stroop task itself, imagine viewing a blue circle on a computer screen. You are asked to identify the color of the shape, not the shape itself. Easy: "Blue." Now you are shown a yellow triangle: "Yellow." Now a red triangle: "Red." The Stroop task is like this, but instead of being shown shapes that are colored, you are shown color words that are colored. For example, you may be shown the word BLUE. The ink color in this book is black, but on the computer screen the color of the word BLUE might be blue or green or red or yellow, etc.

What is interesting about this task is that when a color is attached to a color word rather than a shape, your reaction time changes in one of two directions. If the color word and the color are mismatched, say, the letters of the word BLUE appear in red, your reaction time will be slower than if it were a red shape because your default (dominant) reaction is to read the word rather than identify the color. In order to identify the color, you have to suppress the impulse to read the word, and that takes time, slowing down your reaction. In other words, the impulse to read interferes with the attempt to identify the color. Cognitive psychologists call this the *interference effect*.

What's even more interesting is that when the color and the word match, your reaction time will be faster than with the colored shapes. This is called the *facilitation effect*.

Now suppose you are hypnotized, and the suggestion is that you are no longer literate—you can no longer read. The ability to read is, no doubt, a very important part of your self. I am sure you consider the ability to read to be a key feature of who you are. If you woke up tomorrow and couldn't read any more, you would think that you had lost a very important part of yourself. Some clever scientists did just this. They hypnotized people, implanted a suggestion of illiteracy, and then had them do the Stroop task.[12] What happened? The interference effect went away entirely. It was just as if the hypnotized subjects were looking at shapes instead of color words.

What does this mean for us? Being unable to read the words means the interference effect was no longer a factor, which means that their reaction times in identifying the colors improved. Being unable to read, they did better on the task than when they were able to read.

With the ability removed from their normal cognitive-affective repertoire, the Φ-self of the subjects was diminished in a significant way.

Remember what the Φ-self is. It is the part of us that is aware of what we are doing and feels like it is controlling our action. You may be thinking that because the feeling of overt control in identifying the color was still there, then we should still attribute responsibility to the Φ-self. Consider one other element of this experiment. The facilitation effect did not entirely go away. When the hypnotized subjects identified color words that matched the word in which the colors they were presented, their reaction times were faster than for words where the colors did not match.[13] This means that even though the subjects felt like they were not reading the words, there was still reading going on—but it was selective reading, done only to improve performance and not to impede performance. We can still praise the person for doing better, but the credit should go to the C-self, not the Φ-self, since the subjects are unaware that they are selectively reading.

Is this hypnotized Stroop task a case of natural human action? It seems clear in this case that criterion 2 is met: we can ascribe responsibility in terms of praising the person for doing better than normal, and so it is action in that sense. But what about criterion 1? Was it the Φ-self or the C-self that was responsible? In my opinion, it was the C-self, and so in my opinion, this is, indeed, a case of natural human action.

You may still be skeptical. Maybe it really wasn't action, or maybe the Φ-self was significantly involved. Not to worry, there are other psychological states of Φ-self deficit that we can consider in our search for natural human action. In addition to sleepwalking and hypnosis, there are:

- Inebriation
- Dizziness
- Dreaming
- Adrenaline rush
- Daydreaming
- Schizophrenia
- Psychotropic drugs

You can probably think of even more. Consider examples of behavior performed in any of these states of mind. To what extent is the Φ-self diminished? To the extent that the C-self is dominant? If the C-self is dominant, might the behavior rise to the level of genuine action? There does seem to be one state of mind that gives us a clear-cut case of this. It is the phenomenon of autotelic experience, commonly known as flow, or being in the zone.

We'll look at this state of mind from two perspectives. The first is from the work of Nikolaj Dobrynin. He was a scientist in the Soviet Union who studied attention in the 1920s–1950s. He distinguished three different kinds of attention. In the West, we learn of only two different kinds of attention: voluntary and involuntary. If you studied psychology in the Soviet Union, you would have learned about a third kind of attention, which is still in psychology textbooks in Russia today and in some textbooks in China (just not in textbooks translated from English).[14]

I'm sure you are aware of involuntary attention—when attention is drawn by an external stimulus. Suppose the door closes suddenly, creating a loud sound. You would *involuntarily* turn your head to attend to what was happening there. Voluntary attention, on the other hand, occurs when we direct our attention, due to an internal impetus, toward an intended goal. When you study for a test, this is a good example of voluntary attention. You have to keep renewing your attention and directing yourself toward the subject matter. You're *paying* attention.

What Dobrynin noticed is that students do this a lot, and because it requires effort, they are reticent to do it. He also noticed that students also pay attention when they are playing games. They play very close attention when they are playing games. He noticed, however, that it is a different kind of attention.

When a child plays a game, the attention is neither purely involuntary (drawn by an external stimulus) nor purely voluntary (effortfully directed toward an intended goal). Instead, it seems to be a combination of the two. It begins with voluntary attention, when the child learns the rules of the game and begins to play. This can be a slow, difficult process that requires effortful attention. As the child gains a facility with the rules and ways of the game, it becomes easier, and the child is drawn into the activity. This is where voluntary attention shifts to what Dobrynin calls *postvoluntary attention*. In postvoluntary attention, you are both drawn to something external and your attention is goal-directed. Because it is drawn, it no longer feels effortful, and so maintaining it is not difficult. This is why a student can do homework for only a short time without feeling fatigued but can play a game seemingly endlessly. Dobrynin wondered whether this postvoluntary attention could be harnessed for educational purposes. Unfortunately, this idea has not made its way to the West and so no one has really studied it outside of Russia (and China).

However, in the United States the researcher Mihaly Csikszentmihalyi has studied something similar. In a completely unrelated research program, he developed a theory of what he calls autotelic experience, or flow. According to Csikszentmihalyi, a flow experience has all of the following characteristics:

- Altered sense of time

- High level of concentration

- Confidence and comfort in meeting each new high challenge

- Absence of felt effort

- Absence of self-consciousness

Usually, the altered sense of time is experienced as a slowing of the passage of time. Have you ever, for example, had a great conversation where it felt as though twenty minutes had passed but it had really been more like two hours? That's what Csikszentmihalyi means by an altered sense of time.

Flow also involves a high level of concentration. This is one of the most neglected aspects of flow, even by people who should know better. If you are ever thinking of an experience that you think might be flow-like and you also think that it involves the mind wandering, then it is not a flow experience. Flow necessarily involves a high level of concentration, although it may not *feel* like intense concentration.

A flow experience often involves a high level of skill, and one you are good at, so that when something difficult occurs, you are able to meet that demand confidently. You are also able to meet that demand with such great facility that it feels effortless.

Finally, and this is the one that matters most to us at moment, there is an absence of self-consciousness, meaning that although you are performing the task, it seems in a way divorced from you personally.

Csikszentmihalyi initially studied artists, and so many of them reported a similar kind of detached, flowing experience, that he was able to begin to piece together his theory. Then he discovered it in a wide variety of activities, including playing chess, rock climbing, playing sports, and playing musical instruments. In sports, you often hear it referred to as "being in the zone." I have a friend who is a professional pianist who very much wants to be in this state when he is performing on stage. This attitude is not unusual for musicians, or athletes—because it seems that people tend to perform at their best when in a state of flow. In fact, there are people whose profession it is to help others achieve this state—although it is elusive and seemingly impossible to elicit on demand.

Flow experience is relevant here because it appears to be a state in which the Φ-self blinks out, leaving only the C-self in control. Consider the following quotations from rock climbers that Csikszentmihalyi interviewed:

- "You don't feel like you're doing something as a conscious being; you're adapting to the rock and becoming part of it."

- "You're so involved in what you're doing [that] you aren't thinking about yourself as separate from the immediate activity."

- "Somehow the right thing is done without you ever thinking about it or doing anything at all. . . . It just happens. And yet you're more concentrated."

- "The right decisions are made, but not rationally. Your mind is shut down and your body just goes."[15]

"It just happens." We came across that idea in chapter 1 when we were talking about *ziran*, or *wu wei*. Things were described as occurring "of their own accord." This is self-organization at different levels—at the level of the human individual (rock climbers) and at the level of society. So for the rock climbers, it looks as if the C-self is doing the rock climbing. "Your mind shuts down and your body just goes"—that seems to be a description of the Φ-self going away.

It is worth stating here that in these interviews, Csikszentmihalyi did not first explain his ideas to his subjects and then ask them if they had experienced what he was talking about. Rather, as any good scientist would, he merely asked them to describe their experiences, justifying his work on a vague pretext. It was only after compiling and examining many such interviews that patterns started to emerge, and he was able to piece together a theory.

What do we have in the case of autotelic experience? In the case of sleepwalking, it looked clearly as if we met the first criterion of the Φ-self going away, but the activities failed to rise to the level of genuine action. In the case of hypnosis, the improved performance suggested that it was action, but I imagine some readers are not convinced that the C-self was entirely in the driver's seat. For autotelic experience—or flow, or being in the zone, whatever you want to call it—it seems pretty clear that both criteria have been met: the Φ-self goes away, the C-self is performing the motions, and the motions are performed at such a high level it seems impossible not to attribute responsibility.

I suspect there might be some readers who would argue that if a piano player claims that it "felt like the piano was playing itself," then the pianist doesn't deserve credit, but it's hard to see how that objection would stand up to scrutiny. After all, if you don't give credit to the pianist, who does get the credit for the performance? Imagine a tennis player who is in the zone for the whole match and crushes the opponent. Do we say, "Sorry, you don't get the trophy because your Φ-self wasn't there"? It seems to be distinct from, say, the sleepwalking murder defense. We'll see in the following chapter how the case of flow exposes new boundaries in the cognitive science of action and awareness. Prior to considering flow, it seemed to us impossible to be aware and yet not have a sense of self. But the phenomenon of autotelicity shows us that we can be in full possession of our senses, in command of our actions at a very high level, and yet feel as if the self is absent.

It is not as if the action feels out of control. Recall that one of the criteria of flow above is that one feel in control, but it's not a feeling of *overt* control, just a feeling that whatever occurrence arises is smoothly handled as needed. "Being in control" in this case means not being out of control, not even a little. I have never snow skied before, but I like to think that being in flow is like an expert skier speeding downhill and hitting every mogul just right. The activity carries you along, and you meet every demand in the moment, but you don't feel as if you are moving in a deliberate way. It just happens.

In the case of autotelicity, I submit that we have now solved the paradoxes that troubled us above. We have found a genuine case of natural human action. If C-self action is natural, as I proposed above, then autotelicity is a case of natural action. We have closed the gap between the human and the natural.

Conclusion

To summarize, we have taken the idea of self-organization from physics, where it is a common way of referring to motion in nature, and applied it to the human being, a fundamentally natural creature that operates at virtually every level on the principles of self-organization. There should be nothing controversial about this move. In the process, we have isolated a kind of human movement that can be characterized as natural, namely, movement that occurs in autotelic experience. If you have felt it yourself or witnessed it in others, characterizing it as natural—literally, not just metaphorically—should also not be controversial.

Since the boundary of the human is no longer the boundary of the artificial, it is now also possible to say that there can be artifice in nature. It is when the individual feels as if they are directing the action overtly from a single source of what philosophers call "the will," through volition, or intention, or whatever you want to call that mental act. Does this also happen in nonhuman animals? Since we cannot get into the mind of an animal, it's hard to say for certain. But from observable behavior, as in the bowerbird, it seems possible. At least now, since we have shifted the boundaries of nature and artifice, it seems uncontroversial to study the possibility further.

Let's bring the main point of this chapter to a conclusion.

We began with the paradox of spontaneity:

1. Motion is spontaneous in that it is part of nature.

2. Motion is spontaneous in that it is separate from nature.

This is something that grew out of an examination of Western philosophy in the search for an equivalent of the Chinese notion of *ziran*. But we also discovered that the philosophy of action has its own long-standing paradox, which is largely ignored by philosophers. It goes like this:

1. Natural action is impossible in humans because action to which we can ascribe responsibility is outside of natural law.

2. Human action has to be natural because humans are fundamentally natural creatures.

As it turns out, these paradoxes are actually two ways of saying the same thing: the boundary of the human is the boundary of nature on the outside and artifice on the inside. In the paradox of spontaneity, the second premise is false. In the paradox of natural human action, the first premise if false. The error in both is to view human action as arising from a single point of volition. Rather, it arises through the self-organized cooperation of many disparate parts.

The real question for philosophers of action is why it feels as if there is a single point of volition. We *know* there is plural interaction, yet we *feel* there is monadic volition. So we should not be asking *whether* there can be natural human action, or worse, ruling out the possibility entirely. We should be asking where artifice comes from. Why do we *feel* that we could be separate from nature? The Aristotelian demands it in order to be able to ascribe responsibility under the assumption that natural human motion must be in some way deterministic. This assumption seems far from established, however. It seems just as likely that a strictly deterministic view of natural motion at the level of human action is oversimplified.

Chapter 3

Effortless Attention

A Missing Concept in Contemporary Cognitive Science

In the first chapter, I introduced the concept of *ziran* from traditional Chinese philosophy and attempted to identify some equivalent concepts in Western philosophy. In the second chapter, I looked at some of the consequences of the absence of that concept in the West, one of which was a paradox in the philosophy of action in which the human being is separated from nature. I showed that under the Western paradigm it is impossible to coherently talk about natural human action. Then I attempted to import the idea of *ziran* into current philosophy of action to show how that paradox can be resolved.

In this chapter, I shall do something similar but instead of the field of philosophy, I shall move to the field of cognitive science and show how there is a paradigm in cognitive science[1] that is an inheritance of Western intellectual history, where, again, we lack the concept *ziran*. As a result, there is a gap in our theory. I will again import the idea of *ziran* to show how that gap can be filled.

Let me just back up to the very first chapter and remind you what I'm trying to do overall. The main idea of this book is that in modern universities, our subjects generally come from the Western intellectual tradition. The chemists, the biologists, the neurologists who write our textbooks, even if the textbook is written by Chinese in China, generally come out of the Western tradition, and so they are inheriting some of the presuppositions of the Western tradition. This in itself is not a terrible thing. We've had great advances in society because of this. But every tradition has its limits stemming from its linguistic and cultural forms. Other traditions have thought a lot about the human condition and about the various phenomena that confront us every day, and so if we can examine those traditions carefully, we can gain some insights from them. At the same time, we should examine the Western tradition to see what it lacks, or what it may take for granted, or what it may not be able to see due to its linguistic and cultural forms; then we can help make theory and society better by bringing the strengths of different traditions together.

In this chapter, I take what many people think to be one of the most advanced sciences—the science of the brain—and show how a very old idea from China can improve it. This might sound impossible, but I think by the end of the chapter, you'll be convinced that not only can it be done, it is now in the process of being done.

Effortful and Effortless Attention

Daniel Kahneman is one of the most famous psychologists in the United States, having won the Nobel Prize in Economics and written a best-seller on how people think. He is known for his economic theory about how people tend to make poor judgments when it comes to economic decision making. Before he became famous in economics and decision making, he spent a decade working on the topic of attention, which culminated in the 1973 book *Attention and Effort*. That was a long time ago, but the book is still relevant today. In fact, it helped set the paradigm for how attention has been studied for the last fifty years. In this book, Kahneman associates attention with effort. In fact, he says that attention and effort are the same thing, that when you attend to something you are necessarily exerting effort, and if you are exerting effort in thought, you are necessarily attending to something—there is no difference between the two. Pause for a moment to think about it and see if you agree.

Figure 3.1 is a graph that I created to show how cognitive scientists generally think of effort/attention in response to the demands of a task. Suppose you are doing an addition task that is 2 + 2. That would fall in the lower left of the chart—low demand, low effort. If you continue the

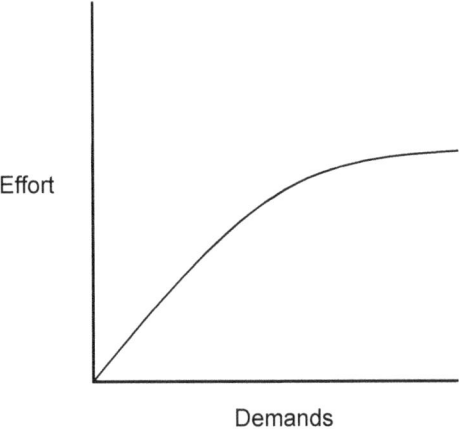

Figure 3.1. Effort increases in response to demands until it can increase no more.

addition task with increasingly large numbers, the demands go higher and higher. As the demands go up, your effort, as long as you continue doing the task, will naturally go up to keep up with the demands. This is something Kahneman discusses in the book—we don't really have a choice about how much effort to put in. If we want to continue the activity, we have to meet the demands, and so our effort will increase accordingly. Because effort and attention are the same for him, we could replace the word *effort* in the chart with *attention*.

To many people, this chart seems intuitively correct. Attending to a task allows us to accomplish something, and any such process requires effort. Think, for example, of some of the slogans we have in English. "If at first you don't succeed, try, try again." "To double your gain, you have to triple your effort," which means that by trying harder, you get more out of it. "Effort is the best indicator of interest," meaning that the more you're interested in something, the more effort you're willing to put into it. Here are some others that I found just searching the Web:

- For every disciplined effort, there is a multiple reward.
- It's all about the effort.
- Work hard to get good, then work hard to get better.

These two things seem to go together. By putting in effort, we get something out of it, attention and effort are inseparable. You cannot put effort into something without paying attention to it.

It's hard to do science without being able to measure what you are studying. And if you cannot measure it directly, you need to figure out a way to measure it indirectly. As it turns out, there is no direct way to measure either attention or effort. There was no way in Kahneman's day and even today it is a huge challenge. As an indirect way to measure effort, Kahneman turned to pupil dilation.[2]

The pupil is the black part of your eye, the center of your eye, which lets the light in. It is, in fact, an aperture, like on a camera. It naturally grows in darkness—to let more light in—and shrinks in bright light—to prevent too much light from getting in. The scientific words for growing larger and shrinking are *dilating* and *contracting*, respectively.

Have you ever seen somebody open their eyes wide when trying to pay attention? Something like that happens involuntarily in the center of your eye. I said it happens when you try harder. We don't actually know why it happens. We just know that there is a correlation, such that when a task gets more difficult and you remain engaged in it, your pupil dilates that much more. The harder the task, the bigger your pupil gets. It's a very interesting phenomenon. You can try it at home looking in the mirror while doing math problems in your head. There is a wrinkle here, however. It also happens when you think about somebody you love. Pupil dilation is not purely a reaction related to cognitive effort; there is also an emotional component.

Although we don't know the direct path of causation from thinking hard to the pupil dilating, we do know that pupil dilation occurs during sympathetic dominance of the autonomic nervous system. We also know that trying hard in cognitive tasks is associated with sympathetic dominance.

Before going farther, let me make sure you understand the concept of sympathetic dominance. In high school biology class, you probably studied the autonomic nervous system, though you probably have only a vague memory of it. Our *peripheral* nervous system is what we use when we see things, hear things, and touch things. It contains the nerves that reach out into our hands and our senses. The *autonomic* nervous system controls the stuff farther inside of us: our liver, our heart, our glands, and all other internal organs.

There are two aspects to the autonomic nervous system. On the righthand side of Figure 3.2, we see a depiction of the elements of

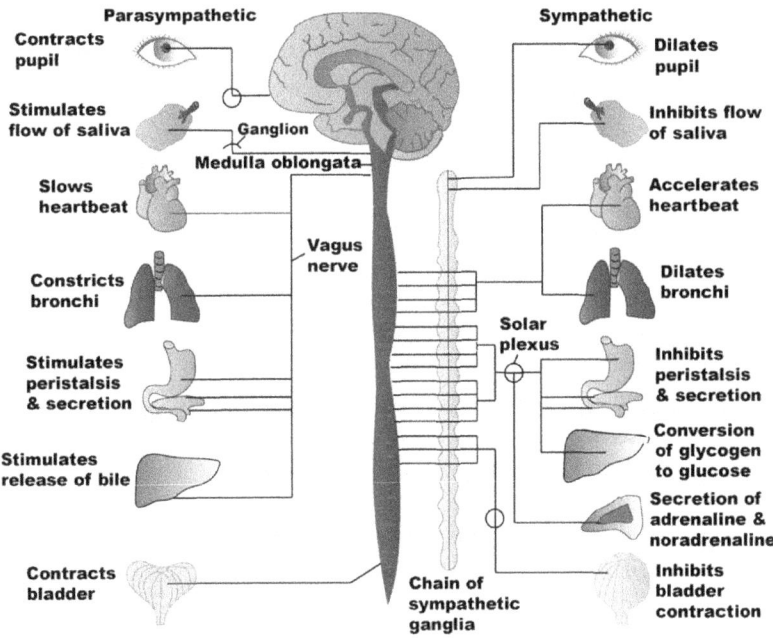

Figure 3.2. Two sides of the autonomic nervous system.

the *sympathetic* autonomic nervous system. On the lefthand side is the *parasympathetic* autonomic nervous system. In normal day-to-day life, when you are neither particularly stressed nor particularly relaxed, these systems play nicely together in a give-and-take relationship that keeps our internal systems functioning in a balanced way. However, there are times when each system coordinates functions particular to it and blocks the functions of the other system. This allows for more efficient functioning toward particular ends.

You may have heard of the fight-or-flight response. This occurs when the sympathetic nervous system is dominant. Sympathetic dominance occurs in a range of situations, from work stress, to fear of loss, to life-or-death struggles for survival. You can see from the righthand side of Figure 3.2 what happens under sympathetic dominance. The pupils dilate, you don't produce saliva in your mouth, your heart beats faster, your lungs can take more air, and so on. So, when Kahneman uses pupil dilation as a measure of attention/effort, he is referring to a reaction of not just the pupils but to a reaction of the whole sympathetic response of the autonomic nervous system, one part of which is pupil dilation. Generally speaking, when any one of these responses occurs consistently over time, the others occur as well. These responses come together as a package.

Parasympathetic dominance of the nervous system is more or less the opposite of sympathetic dominance. It is called the *rest and digest* response. When it is dominant, your pupils contract, you produce more saliva (this is generally when you eat), your heartbeat slows down, you don't have as much capacity for breathing, your stomach and your intestines are at full digestive functioning, etc.

In the second chapter, I gave you an example of a common task in cognitive science called the Stroop task. In the Stroop task, you are presented with a color word (such as BLUE or RED) on the screen and are instructed to identify the color of the print of the word, not the word itself. Your first response, your dominant response, will be to read the word. What the Stroop task forces you to do is suppress that dominant response, which is difficult and so requires effort. You have to really pay attention. The more rapidly the words are flashed, the more you have to pay attention. This and similar tasks are used in the laboratory to test attention and also to study what occurs in the body while paying attention.

According to Kahneman, attention equals effort, and effort is indexed by activation of the sympathetic autonomic nervous system, that is, sympathetic dominance—pupil dilation, increased heart rate, etc. But this is where it gets interesting. It's not actually always the case that when you are paying attention to something, all parts of the sympathetic nervous system work together. Sometimes, for example, the pupils may dilate, but the heart rate doesn't increase. This is called fractionation, as opposed to dominance. Things kind of break apart. There is not a unified response by the autonomic nervous system. So because Kahneman's theory is that attention is underpinned by the sympathetic autonomic nervous system, this kind of event (fractionation) can be regarded as a counterexample.

An important question for a scientist is: When you encounter an anomaly in the evidence, when you have data that don't match up with your theory, what do you do? I think this is a classic example of what Thomas Kuhn talked about in his famous book, *The Structure of Scientific Revolutions*. In his book, Kuhn looked at examples of scientific paradigms over the centuries and what happened when anomalous results occurred. How did the theorists respond? What he found is that people, even scientists, make excuses and try to fit the theory to the results, instead of questioning the theory fundamentally. The first instinct of a dogmatic scientist is that the theory is correct. So, if there are data that don't fit the theory, the data are often just ignored or the theory is tweaked a little bit to accommodate the data.

What did Kahneman do when he was faced with this kind of anomalous result? He said that it doesn't count as attention. He redefined attention in three different aspects and said, if it's not a case of sympathetic dominance, it's not genuine attention. Genuine attention occurs only when there is sympathetic dominance signifying effort.

There exists only one published review of Kahneman's book. In the review, this data anomaly is not commented on. Even the major people working in the field alongside Kahneman let this slip, and it is an indication, I think, that there is something more going on—that this paradigm is so deeply engrained that it is hard to spot an anomaly when it arises.

How Kahneman dealt with fractionation is an indication that there might be something wrong with the theory that attention just is effort. Another indication is the fact that Kahneman never defined his notion of effort. He began the book by talking about energy. Then he stopped talking about energy and started talking about effort, suggesting that by effort, he means expenditure of energy. But what exactly does that mean? The brain is constantly metabolizing, constantly using energy. How is attention distinct from normal energy expenditure?

The fact is, we don't know exactly what is happening in our brains when we're trying hard. Probably there is some kind of energy consumption, some kind of metabolic process. But what is it in comparison to what we're doing when we're not paying attention? We don't know.

One way to understand effort in human cognition is to begin with the notion of effort in physics, where there is a well-established theory. We all have experiences of lifting something heavy or riding a bike up a hill. We know that the steeper the hill, the more effort we have to put into riding up it, or the heavier the thing, the more effort we have to put into lifting it. In the terms used in physics, we say that an increase in load requires an increase in effort.

The full theory in physics is much more complex than just this, but we can move from this little bit of theory to human physiology, the study of how the body works. In physiology we can separate effort into two kinds. Objective effort is the amount of effort it takes to do something. There is also subjective effort—the feeling of how hard it is to do something. If I'm picking up, say, a fifty-pound bag of potatoes, it would feel hard for me, but for a weightlifter it would feel less hard because he (or she) has lots of well-practiced muscles. Although the objective effort is the same in these two cases, the subjective effort is different.

In the 1960s, the physiologist Gunnar Borg put people on treadmills and then strapped them to heart monitors and respiration monitors to see how much they were exerting in terms of their physiological responses. Then he asked them how much they *felt* they were exerting? He found that there was a good correlation between the two, that people were good at saying how much effort they were putting out. The subjective scale that Borg developed is still used today by people who study human physiology. So if you want to know how much objective physiological effort somebody is putting out in the laboratory or in the doctor's office, you don't need the machines, you can just ask the person doing it. It saves a lot of time and resources.

There is another interesting thing about effort—namely, that we can use tools to reduce effort. If we want to move a rock that weighs a thousand pounds, we cannot do it by brute force alone. But we can do it with the use of tools, such as levers and pulleys, that reduce the amount of effort we have to put in to exert a higher effort on the load. In combined physics and physiological terms, we can say that we exert high objective effort with low subjective effort.

This is what we know about physics and physiology. In the realm of cognition, to what extent are these ideas relevant? I am raising this question not because this is how cognitive scientists do it, but because I think we need to think more clearly about what effort fundamentally is. Cognitive scientists haven't done this work yet. They just presume to know what effort it is. There is talk about effort, but few have tried to define it.[3]

So what can we say about effort in cognition? We know that there is something we might call subjective effort in cognition. All of us feel something happening when we're trying hard to do a math problem or to pay attention to a difficult set of ideas in a long argument. But we don't know what is going on in the brain when we feel subjective effort. It is mostly a mystery.

Objective cognitive effort is also a mystery. We don't have pulleys or levers in the brain. We have nerves and blood vessels and neurotransmitters, but we don't know what changes exactly when we're putting in effort. And we don't have any way of knowing if when we feel like we're putting in more effort, we are actually putting in more effort. Could it be that these two things are different or that we're not good at estimating cognitive effort? Or maybe, like in physiology, we are very good at it. We just don't know because there is currently no way to measure objective cognitive effort.

It makes sense intuitively to think that there is a correlation between what we feel and what we do when we engage in a difficult task. But even these seem to be neurologically dissociable. Lionel Naccache, a cognitive scientist and neurologist in France, had a patient who had brain damage in one particular part of her brain. Naccache and his team had her do cognitive tasks, like the Stroop task, and as the tasks got harder, the patient was able to do them like any normal person. But when they asked the patient if it was more difficult, she couldn't say. She had no feeling of subjective effort, presumably because that particular part of her brain was damaged.[4] This suggests that objective cognitive effort and subjective cognitive effort have distinct brain architectures, that they are not one and the same thing. There seems to be a physiological aspect of our brain that registers what we are doing and how effortful it feels. If that part goes down, then we don't have the feeling of effort.

Kahneman did not distinguish between subjective and objective effort. He said that attention equals effort, and implied that effort equals objective effort, which is indexed by the sympathetic autonomic nervous system. Although he alluded to subjective effort, he seemed to view it as the same thing as objective effort.

Is it possible that there could be attention in a normal person without the feeling of effort? Could there even be an increase in attention with a decrease in objective effort? Are there the equivalent of pulleys and levers in the brain that allow a person to accomplish a difficult task with reduced effort? What about the cases of postvoluntary attention and flow discussed in chapter 2? That kind of concentration seems to be a clear case of high attention and at least low subjective effort. Could it also involve lower objective effort? Kahneman discusses none of this.

According to the current paradigm of attention theory, stemming from Kahneman's work, any reduction in effort while attention remains high is impossible—because attention just is effort. It's like asking if you can have less H_2O but the same amount of water. The answer is no, because H_2O is nothing but water.

However, we know that in human physiology, reducing objective effort (effort force) through pulleys, levers, etc. reduces subjective effort—the feeling of exertion. In human cognition, we know we can reduce subjective effort through games, absorption, etc. Does that mean that we have also reduced objective effort? What does it mean if a difficult cognitive task feels easier? Does it mean that there is less of whatever effort is? Suppose it is energy expenditure—does that mean we're spending less energy on it? Think of, say, a math game. Is it easier to do math as part of a game than just math problems on a page? If it feels easier, does that mean there's actually less energy being spent? This is something we don't know. What we do know is that it is not theoretically impossible. We also know that there seems to be sufficient evidence to say at the very least that attention does not equal subjective effort.

What I'm trying to get at here is that although there has been a lot of research in psychology done on attention over the past sixty or seventy years, because the paradigm has been that attention equals effort—even before Kahneman published his book, this was the reigning paradigm though not clearly stated—there seems to be the possibility that the paradigm is flawed. In the remaining part of this chapter, I will demonstrate that there is a pretty strong probability that attention not only does not equal subjective effort but also does not equal objective effort either.

Let me take you back for a moment to the first chapter. There, I introduced the basic idea of the Chinese notion of *ziran*. To recap, this idea comes basically from the *Zhuangzi* and the *Laozi* from around twenty-three to twenty-five hundred years ago. I focused on this as a theory of ideal action and approached it from three aspects. The English name I gave to it was *spontaneity*, or the adverb *naturally*, but the Chinese words are *ziran* and *wu wei*. I suggested that the *zi* of *ziran* is doing most of the work in that idea, and it means that the action is coming from internal resources, not external resources, that there is no interference from outside, and most importantly, there is a kind of what I call multivalent causality. So instead of a central will commanding the action, there is multivalence—all parts of the body, or many parts of the body, and mind working together. A convenient phrasing we saw in English was that something happens *of its own accord*. This was D. C. Lau's nice translation of *ziran*.

In the case of *wu wei*, we saw that it can be characterized as an absence of direct intentionality. You may be doing something very difficult, but as long as you are not *trying* to do it, as long as you are not putting overt, intentional effort into it, it is *wu wei*.

The idea of spontaneity / *wu wei* is illustrated in skill stories that we saw in *Zhuangzi*. There I tried to show some representative stories and break down the psychology of *ziran* / *wu wei* into the two basic ideas of wholeness and fluency. For wholeness, there is a concentration, which is a high level of attention and collection of energies focused on a single task. Think of any kind of skill that you have learned and how when you are doing this skill in a context of high challenge, you become totally concentrated on it. This is what we saw in those stories. We also saw skilled people in the stories, when asked how they did it, saying that it involved a high level of concentration, but also a *letting go*, which means getting rid of distractions, setting things aside, such as your own self-worth or your own self-concerns.

The idea of fluency has to do with one's actions. Fluent actions are responsive. Although the skilled person may be doing something difficult, the person can respond effectively to whatever might arise in that context. Fluency also involves a feeling of ease, that although what one is doing might be technically difficult, there is not the feeling that one is having trouble with it. There is a feeling of command over the circumstances. In other words, it can feel controlled but effortless.

This is the basic idea of *ziran* and the kind of idealized action that we see in Daoism. The idea is largely missing in traditional Western philosophy. And I think, as you can see, because there's both a high level of concentration and a feeling of ease, this idea directly contradicts the reigning paradigm in the cognitive science of attention.

I was first exposed to this Daoist idea as a high school student, reading books from my local library about Eastern philosophy. Then I studied it formally as an undergraduate in Chinese Philosophy class. Later, I researched it while writing my PhD dissertation, when I also began studying attention. As a professor, I looked more closely at attention, which is when I realized that there is a problem with the current theory. It occurred to me that maybe this idea from Daoism can help us understand attention better.

But I'm not the only one who has had ideas about effortless attention. There actually have been some scientists who looked at what we might call in retrospect effortless attention. For example, I mentioned in the second chapter the Russian psychologist Nikolaj Dobrynin. Dobrynin gave us the idea of *postvoluntary attention*.

To recap, Dobrynin was interested in trying to help students learn better because paying voluntary attention is hard for them. He saw that when they play games, they could be paying very high attention to something but be perfectly fine with it. What if we could make education less effortful? What would that mean? The idea of postvoluntary attention is important because unlike in a laboratory and unlike in an unexpected event, your attention is drawn by the subject matter, as when a game draws you in, but it is also goal directed, like voluntary attention.

Unfortunately, Dobrynin's work is very little known. If you ask any Western cognitive scientist about it today, it will be very hard to find even one who has heard of postvoluntary attention. Dobrynin did his work in the first part of the twentieth century in Russia, and only a very small portion of it has been translated into English. However, if you ask an older Chinese cognitive scientist, they might say they've heard of it because they've been exposed to Russian psychology theories. Still, it is outside of mainstream cognitive science today, even in China.

Mihaly Csikszentmihalyi is an American psychologist, and the one who is responsible for giving us the theory of flow, or what some call being in the zone. Csikszentmihalyi also called it autotelic experience. In chapter 2, we saw that this is when you are highly engaged in a task, such as playing a musical instrument or weightlifting or playing a sport, and you lose yourself in it—that is, you become fully absorbed in it. You are able to accomplish the demands that are put in front of you, and it doesn't feel difficult. There is a loss of the normal sense of time and an absence of self-consciousness. These are the basic constituents of flow, or autotelic experience, according to Csikszentmihalyi. If any one of these is missing, it does not count as flow. For example, suppose you are driving down a quiet street or walking through a peaceful garden. You might experience some of the constituents of flow, like a sense of automaticity or a loss of a normal sense of time, but most likely you will not be highly attentive to the task of driving or walking. Without high attention, it doesn't count as flow.

To my surprise, I found in my research that the work of neither Dobrynin nor Csikszentmihalyi had influenced cognitive science to a significant degree. However, there is one perspective from which cognitive scientists have begun to rethink the attention paradigm. That is from studying meditation. Meditation is, by definition, an example of an activity with a high level of attention. When a person is meditating, the meditator is paying attention to something. That's what it means to meditate. There is a wide variety of meditation techniques. A meditator may focus on a mandala, a mantra, on the breath, on thoughts coming and going, etc.

Scientists who have studied meditation have discovered that during meditation, subjects can experience a lower heart rate, lower skin conductance, a lower respiratory rate, and a higher heart rate variability. All of these are indications of parasympathetic dominance of the autonomic nervous system and so suggest effortlessness as opposed to the signs of effort associated with sympathetic dominance.

The combination of high attention in meditation along with parasympathetic response appears to be proof that we can have high attention without sympathetic dominance. It may also mean that we can have high attention and low objective effort.

In 2010, I published the edited volume *Effortless Attention*. Prior to that, I had an opportunity to work with Csikszentmihalyi for six weeks on a project at the University of Pennsylvania. I brought my Chinese background into it because he was interested in that. The project was to reconsider the idea of flow with respect to the new field of positive psychology. As part of that process, I wanted to know more about the science of flow. So I went to the library at the University of Pennsylvania to find all the information I could about what cognitive scientists had said about his theory, and I found next to nothing. He'd been working on his theory for three decades and published books and articles about it. But (this is my opinion) because it didn't match the reigning paradigm in cognitive science, very few cognitive scientists had taken it seriously or found it worth studying. And so I thought that, as part of that project, I would expand my view of cognitive science and try to understand various cognitive aspects of effortless attention to see what scientists were doing that might shed some light on effortlessness. Then I would invite them to write an article for the book. If they were studying flow or if they wanted to think more about flow or take flow seriously as a subject in cognitive science, what might they say?

I was surprised by the positive response I got from some very accomplished scientists. And so we put together a book, and it was published by MIT Press. For any skeptics out there, this should be pretty good evidence that it is possible to take a very old Chinese idea and import it into contemporary theory. There is not only the MIT book. The American Psychological Association puts out a dictionary that undergoes revision on a regular basis. After the *Effortless Attention* book came out, the dictionary added an entry on effortless attention, so one can now say that the idea has officially entered the field.

One of the authors of one of the articles in the book was a scholar named Yiyuan Tang, who got his PhD in China and is now a professor of cognitive psychology in the United States. He and I have started collaborating on trying to prove empirically that effortless attention is an actual phenomenon. So far, we have published three theoretical papers together. The second paper directly targets Kahneman's theory, demonstrating its weaknesses.

Research on Effortless Attention

So far in this chapter, we have established, on the one hand, that intuitively it can seem right that attention just is effort, as when doing math problems. On the other hand, however, it also seems intuitively right that attention can feel effortless—playing games, for instance, and being in flow. Many questions arise from these two competing intuitions. What exactly is cognitive effort? Is objective cognitive effort different from subjective cognitive effort? Can one be reduced while the other stays the same? What are the neurological and physiological correlates of objective or subjective cognitive effort? If we are to study effortless attention, we can do it from many different aspects. The aspects that were examined in the *Effortless Attention* book are the following:

Expertise

Action Syntax

Decision Making

Mental Training

Effort

Automaticity

Agency

The meaning of each of these in the context of effortless attention is summarized in the Introduction to that book, where I also explain how the articles of the book speak to these aspects. In what follows, I will explain four research projects that have been done on attention and how they suggest that there really is a thing such as effortless attention. I want to do this partially just to show you some of the very cool things going on in cognitive science plausibly related to effortless attention, but also to make a point that effortless attention really is a phenomenon worth deeper examination.

Focus of Attention Affects Performance

Gabriel Wulf, a kinesiologist at the University of Nevada, Las Vegas, has spent two decades studying human movement as it relates to attention. She did an extensive series of experiments that were very simple in their basic setup. When people were doing different kinds of sports, she asked them to pay attention to one of two different aspects of what they were doing. They were instructed to pay attention either to some relevant part of their body or to something outside of themselves but still relevant to the activity. What she found is that things almost always work better when you focus outside of yourself rather than on some part of your body. She used many different kinds of tests, such as testing muscles or just measuring the effects when subjects did certain movements. She found maximum accuracy, power, coordination, and consistency, and a minimum of energy, effort, and time when subjects focused outside of themselves, as opposed to focusing on some part of their body.

    This result is relevant here because it shows that attention and effort are associated such that objective physiological effort can be reduced in an activity by paying attention in a certain way. At least in physiology, then, we see that attention and effort are not so tightly connected that attention necessarily equals effort. If attention did equal effort, you would never see a difference unless it just meant that you were paying more or less attention. (By the way, Kahneman also did not distinguish physiological effort from cognitive effort. One of his examples is effort in running, a sport that Wulf happened to use in her studies.)

    Let me tell you a little about her experiments so that you can get a better sense of her accomplishments and how they relate to effortless attention. In one study, she had subjects do weightlifting curls and measured their muscle activity using an electromyograph, which measures electrical activity in muscles, which gives us a sense of the amount of physiological effort being exerted. She instructed the subjects to either focus their attention on the bar they were lifting or on the arm they were using to lift. She found that focusing on the bar made it objectively easier to do. There was less electrical activity in the muscles when subjects focused on the bar than on their own arm, meaning that the muscles were doing the same amount of work, but less energy was being put into the task.

Another experiment involved vertical jumping. Wulf had people jump directly up and touch rings suspended overhead. Which rings they touched would tell her how high they jumped. She instructed subjects to focus on either the ring they were reaching for or on the fingertips they were using to reach. At the height of the jump, there is not much difference between where the ring is and where your fingertip is, so it seems like there really shouldn't be much of an effect generated by just which you choose to focus on. However, she found that when people focused outside of themselves on the rings, they were able to jump higher (because, as it turns out, they were getting more force out of their jump).

A third study involved long distance running on a treadmill in which the subjects ran at 75 percent of their maximum capacity. Wulf had them focus on either a video of the environment or on some part of their body. When they focused externally, she found that they used less oxygen, had lower blood lactate (produced from muscle activity), and rated it as subjectively easier.

Together, these cases show how a different focus of attention results in a measurable effect on both subjective and objective effort. The change in attention leads to more efficient movement. When the load is constant, less objective effort is required. When maximal effort is exerted, a change in attention results in more force. These are very intriguing results.

For the *Effortless Attention* book, Wulf summarized her work in this area and then speculated about the reason behind these results. She believes that conscious control constrains the motor system (the brain system that controls action) by interfering with automatic processes. When we focus on the body, we ever so slightly begin to exert conscious control, she suggests. This may have to do with a pervading sense of self associated with the body. For this reason, Wulf calls this phenomenon the "self-invoking trigger"—somehow by thinking about our body, we bring the self to consciousness, and that interrupts the automaticity of the actions. This is her speculation. We don't know if it is really the case. It is an area that deserves more exploration.

A Single Coding System for Perception and Movement

Bernhard Hommel, an accomplished cognitive scientist working in Europe, studies what happens in the brain when we are perceiving something, processing the information, and then acting. This is called the perception-action cycle. It is something that is engaged every moment that we're awake.

I think most of us have the impression that before we act, our brain has no activity related to the act, that it is only when we begin the act that our brain begins working on making the action, and then it simply does what we tell it to do. Actually, our brain begins making estimations of what is needed before the movement begins and is constantly calculating and predicting during the course of the movement. Suppose you are going to put pen to paper to write something. From your personal point of view, it's an easy process that requires next to no thought at all. However, your brain has to calculate where exactly to put the pen, the angles and force of movement required to get it there, and how hard to press. It also has to predict what the effects will be during that entire process. For example, it will have to predict how hard and how smooth the writing surface will be. Will the paper move with the pen, or will the paper stay stationary? All these things are going on in your brain, even though you are not thinking about them consciously. Hommel tries to understand that whole process from beginning to end. What exactly are we estimating? How do we do it? What parts of the brain are involved in doing it? And so on.

Hommel says there are basically two fundamental things going on. First, there is action planning. Let's take the pen-to-paper example. It takes three fingers to hold the pen. The surface is horizontal. The pen is more or less vertical. These are general features of the action. He has found that these features are encoded in a processing stream in the ventral part of the brain, which is basically the underside of the brain. There is a constant stream of information going on about the general features of whatever action you're engaging in. But there's also another stream of processing—the dorsal stream that happens at the top of your brain, where the specific parts of the action are being filled in as you are doing them. As the pen is going to the paper, you need to calculate exactly how much pressure to put on it in the specific circumstances. Those amounts are being filled in moment to moment by this upper processing stream.

As you might already have guessed, the ventral processing stream is the more conscious part of the brain, and the dorsal stream is the less conscious part. Thus, we are aware of the general features of our actions, but we're not aware of the moment-to-moment filling in of what's going on in the actions. There is a certain automaticity to that. There is an example of this in the work of Prablanc and Pellison,[5] colleagues of Hommel. They had subjects move one finger from a home position on a computer screen to a spot of light on the same screen. As the finger was moving, and just as the subject blinked, the spot of light changed position slightly. Amazingly, subjects were able to land their finger in the correct spot, without hesitation, and without awareness that an adjustment had been made. According to Hommel, this suggests two cognitive systems at work in movement—a system that is open to consciousness and another that is beneath conscious awareness. It also suggests that whatever kind of coding occurs in the brain is a single kind of code across both perception and action networks.

Figure 3.3 shows the basic features of the two systems and how they work together. The way to read this diagram is to start at the top, where action planning begins. The dark circles represent general features of actions that we control consciously (in the ventral stream). The blank circles represent specific features that remain undetermined until the moment they are needed. Which specific features are chosen is determined by perceptual input beneath consciousness (the dorsal stream).

Hommel says that the implications of his work are that the current action goal coordinates action control processes. So whatever you're trying to do, that's what's controlling what you're doing. When you're putting the pen to the paper, you don't have to think to yourself: "two point five pounds of pressure, up to the right at seventy-five degrees." Instead, you think: "Write the word 'Dear,'" and your brain takes it from there. Action control processes automatically trigger attention processes. When the little bits and pieces are filled in as the action unfolds, your eyes and your perceptions still have to move there, but you may not notice it.

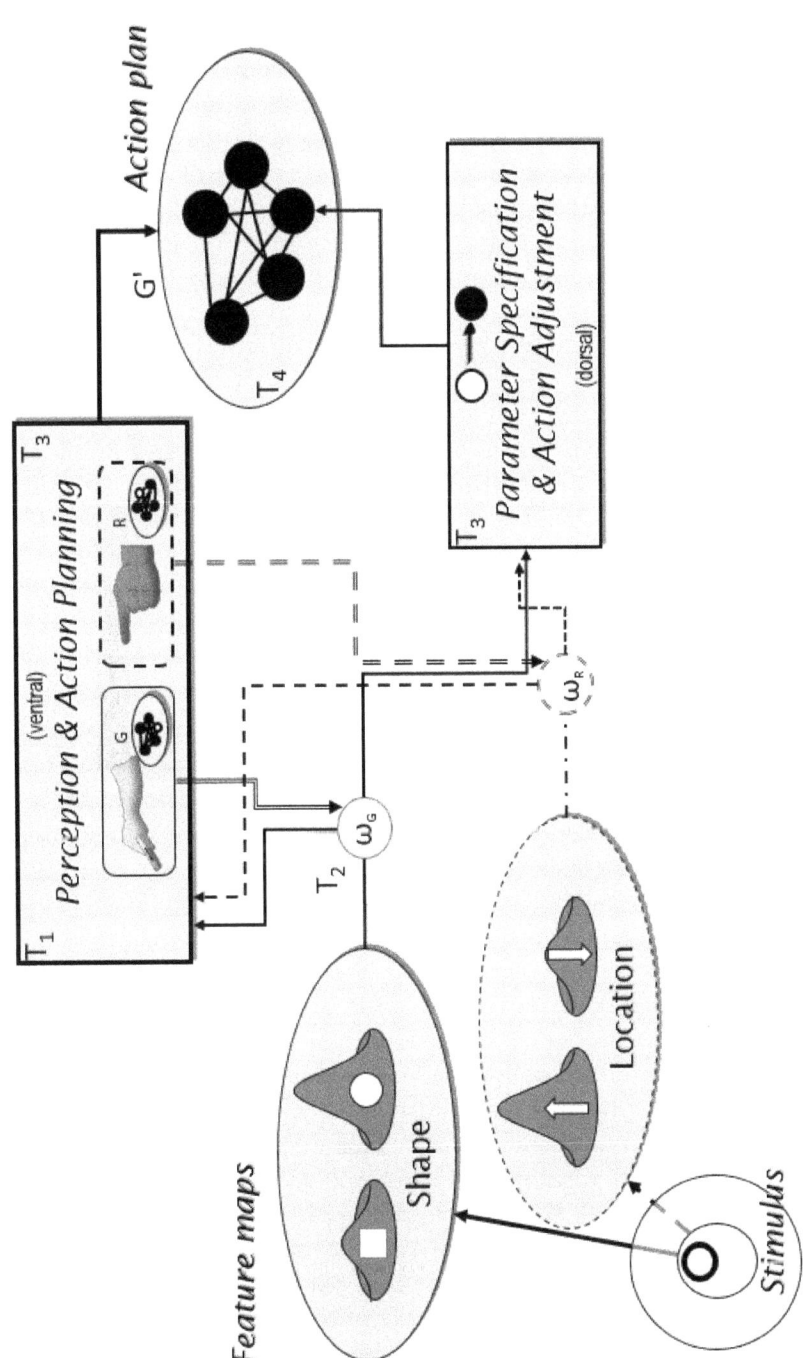

Figure 3.3. Common code of the perception-action cycle.

Thus, Hommel suggests that in our day-to-day activity, when we are walking along the street outside or putting pen to paper, our attention is constantly in use. It is moving from here to there and there to here, but it doesn't feel effortful. He thinks that when we put somebody in a laboratory and we have them do tasks, this is more of an exception to the rule than the rule itself. If you think about it, how much time is actually spent during a day trying to pay attention to something effortfully? It's hard actually to maintain effortful attention for very long.

According to Hommel, if we want to understand attention, we have to understand it under normal circumstances so that we can get a full sense of it. When we put somebody in a laboratory, that's a very different way of acting from how we normally act. We don't usually have somebody pointing at us and saying, "Do this and then do that. You have no interest in it whatsoever, but do it anyway. Just for five minutes." That would be an unusual way to behave out in the real world.

Hommel thinks it is better to think about human action under what is called ecologically valid circumstances—the normal way of doing things. And he thinks the normal way of attention is largely effortless. He says that it is the selection, representation, and maintenance of the action goal that is effortful. He says, "The frequent use of artificial tasks that are not deeply anchored in the participant's motivational structure and not supported by environmental cues have led to a rather drastic over estimation of the cognitive effort needed to deal with everyday life."[6]

Neurological Correlates of Effortless Attention

Matthew Botvinick is a cognitive scientist at Princeton University, where he studies a part of the brain that responds to conflict. Suppose you're putting your pen down on paper to write, and no ink comes out. He studies a part of the brain that would activate when that happens. He takes an economic view of how the brain makes decisions. He says that when choosing a response, high intensity often yields the best results. In other words, trying hard pays off. I think we probably all know this. If you want to get a hundred on a test, you go and study hard for it. And that can pay off. We saw that idea in the very beginning of this chapter. But high intensity also has a cost. We don't know exactly what that cost is in neurophysiological terms, but we do know that after we pay attention for a while, we feel fatigued. Therefore, according to Botvinick, we can conclude that our brain tries to meet the demands necessary but at the lowest cost possible. This just makes sense. This is how biology generally works. Nothing is wasted, everything is optimized.

According to Botvinick and his co-author Joseph McGuire, demand during cognitive tasks is evaluated in terms of response conflict, meaning that when we do something easily, there is not as much conflict as when it is difficult. For example, suppose you put pen to paper and no ink comes out. This is an unexpected situation, a conflict in terms of what you expected to happen. As a result, you might push a little harder. Your brain has noticed the problem and prompted you to exert more conscious control, which you do and which is subjectively felt to be effortful. This is called top-down control. When we do something automatically, that's called bottom-up control.

To get a better sense of this, take a look at Figure 3.4. In Figure 3.4, you see two views of the brain. Your brain has two hemispheres. If you could remove the left hemisphere and look at the right side of the brain from the left, you would see the view on the left side of Figure 3.4, the interior of the brain. The right side of Figure 3.4 is the view of

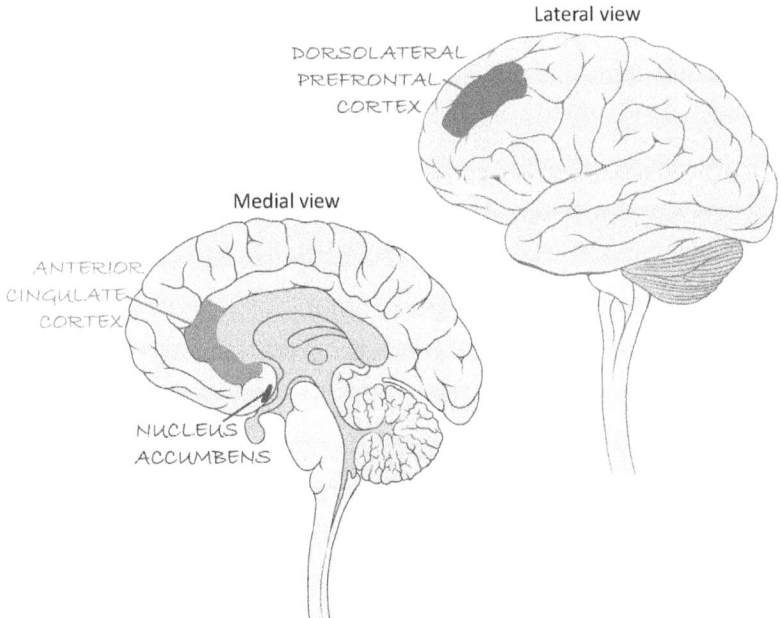

Figure 3.4. Some areas of the brain involved in decision making. Source: Wikimedia Commons.

the left side of the brain, also from the left, so the exterior of the brain.

The part of the brain I was talking about that does the conflict monitoring is the anterior cingulate cortex, or ACC for short. If I am doing an activity but something unexpected happens, just the slightest thing, the ACC kicks in and sends a signal to the dorsolateral prefrontal cortex, or DLPFC for short, to say that something is wrong. In the pen and paper example, if you put the pen to paper and no ink comes out, a signal might go from the ACC to the DLPFC. The DLPFC is the center of what cognitive scientists call executive control, the part of the brain that we might associate with the will. The DLPFC, might then tell the motor system to push harder. In other words, the ACC is constantly monitoring what we are doing, making sure that the effort we're expending is up to the task we are doing.

But that's not all there is to the story. There is another part of your brain called the nucleus accumbens, which encodes how worthwhile it is to do something—in other words, it encodes for prospective reward. Let's suppose you are a little bit hungry but the only food around needs to be cleaned, cut, and cooked before eating, instead of just opening a package and gobbling it down. If you were expecting some prepared food and don't find it, your ACC will go into action, telling your DLPFC that things are not quite right. And your DLPFC will begin to calculate how to rectify the situation. At the same time, your nucleus accumbens is calculating the reward involved. What seems to happen in the DLPFC is that the amount of reward is compared to the amount of effort required, and if the reward is insufficient, the DLPFC backs down, and nothing happens. Only when the reward signal exceeds the effort signal, does the DLPFC take action.

The article I am referring to by McGuire and Botvinick appears in the *Effortless Attention* book, but what does all this have to do with effortless attention? Flow often occurs during activities that are quite challenging, such as playing the violin or rock climbing. Because these activities are difficult, often involving many, tiny unexpected occurrences and adjustments as the activity unfolds, Botvinick's model tells us that the ACC would often be active, telling the DLPFC to kick in, also involving reward calculations from the nucleus accumbens. All of this activity would presumably give the person a feeling of effort. Sometimes, however, even during a challenging activity, everything goes smoothly, and no matter what happens, we are perfectly ready for it. If nothing unexpected happens, the ACC is not active. And if it is not signaling the DLPFC, there will be no need to calculate the effort/reward tradeoff. This, McGuire and Botvinick speculate, is the feeling of being in flow. In flow, it is as if we are perfectly in tune with our activity, even if it is very difficult. Whatever occurs, we are ready for. The brain is also ready, and so no extra output is recruited. From this perspective, perhaps effortless attention is not attention with less overall effort but with less *extra* effort.

Because it is difficult to induce flow in the laboratory, this theory remains speculation for the time being. The overall model involving the ACC, DLPFC, and nucleus accumbens is pretty well established (and much simplified in my retelling of it), but we are not sure how they interact during flow.

Training Attention

Michael Posner, Mary Rothbart, M. R. Yueda, and Yiyuan Tang did some amazing studies of attention in children. Before we get into the studies, let me explain a couple of things. First, through many years of work, Posner (a psychologist, now retired, at the University of Oregon) discovered that there is something he calls the executive attention network that stretches out to different parts of the brain.

Above, we discussed suppressing a dominant response, such as in the Stroop task. A term we can use for that is *effortful control*. Remember, in the Stroop task, the easiest thing to do is to read the word. You have to suppress that response in order to look at the color and identify that color. This is effortful control. Posner and colleagues found that there are certain genes that code for different aspects of the executive attention brain network, that code for effortful control. In other words, it is not the case that we all have the same genes and get the same attentional network. Some of us have slightly different genes, which results in a slightly differently functioning attentional network.

Think, for example, of children who have ADHD. It is hard for such children to pay attention effortfully. Posner and colleagues have found that certain genes are associated with this deficit. But genes are not destiny. Posner and colleagues also found that so-called high quality parenting reduces the influence of these genes. What does this mean? Let's say Bobby is a child who has trouble paying attention effortfully. Scientists find that he has the COMT gene, which reduces the efficiency of his executive attention network. Scientists also bring his parents in and observe how they interact with him, finding that they do not possess good parenting skills. Another child the scientists study, let's say her name is Sally, also has the COMT gene but does not show signs of ADHD. Under observation, the scientists find that her parents have very good parenting skills. These correlations, found over many subjects, suggest that good parenting can help children compensate for faring poorly in the genetic lottery—at least in the narrow case of these genes that code for attention.

Posner and colleagues didn't stop there. They wanted to see if they could also change the behavior of the children by improving their attention through certain cognitive training exercises. They found that they were able to improve a child's ability to pay attention through two very different kinds of exercises. One involved computer task training, in which children control figures on a screen with a joystick, exercising children's abilities of prediction, working memory, and resolving conflict. Posner and colleagues found some very interesting things. There were specific changes after just five to ten days of these computer tasks. There was more activity in the ACC. Remember, that is the part of your brain that does conflict monitoring. One of the problems of these children is that this part isn't always functioning well enough, so they don't know something is not right, making them more impulsive. Posner and colleagues also found something that is supposed to be impossible, namely, an increase in general IQ. And when they tested the children two months later, that improvement was still there. They also found an increase in affective regulation—the ability to wait for reward.

But that's not the only kind of training they did. They also did meditation training with university students. Yiyuan Tang has developed a systematic way of training people in a certain kind of meditation he calls integrative body-mind training, a practice that stems from traditional Chinese medicine. The subjects in the study practiced for twenty minutes per day over five days. Another group of students—the control subjects—did a kind of relaxation training. Posner and colleagues found that Tang's method of meditation practice correlated with an improvement in executive attention, lower negative affect (meaning less irritability), less fatigue, and a lower level of stress.

The results of this series of studies by Posner and colleagues are quite amazing. Even though our attentional abilities are affected by our genes, they can be modulated by the environment in the form of parenting and in the form of cognitive training, including meditation.[7]

This work is consistent with the work above by McGuire and Botvinick and suggests that attention can be improved at the same time cognitive effort is reduced (by improving one's ability of effortful control). If attention were nothing but effort, by contrast, increases or decreases in effort would always result in concomitant increases or decrease in attention. But that is not what we see in these studies. This work is also consistent with the meditation studies I mentioned above that involve parasympathetic dominance. As it turns out, Tang did one of those studies, using the kind of meditation he used here, suggesting again an association between parasympathetic dominance and less effort.

Conclusion

To summarize, I am suggesting in this chapter that attention can be effortless and not merely effortful. We've looked at the topic from the perspectives of flow, postvoluntary attention, and attention in meditation that's associated with parasympathetic dominance. We've looked at Gabriele Wulf's work on external focus and how it increases movement efficiency; at Bernard Hommel's work, in which he shows that moment-to-moment attention might actually be more effortless than we think it is; at McGuire and Botvinick's model of a possible neural mechanism of flow; and at Posner and colleagues' findings that attentional and emotional regulation can be trained.

So how does this chapter connect with the notion of *ziran*? After all, none of these scientists discuss it—they discuss effortless attention. Actually, originally, they discussed neither *ziran* nor effortless attention. They did their work on various aspects of attention, perception, and action. I came across their research as I was conceptualizing what effortless attention as a new concept might entail.

There are a quite a few philosophers working in the cognitive sciences, doing conceptual work—developing new ideas, developing the logic of current theories, seeing things that scientists, who are deeply involved in getting the science right, might miss. So my developing the notion of effortless attention is recognizable as the kind of thing that a philosophers do day in and day out.

But where does the idea of *ziran* come in? *Ziran* is what got me going in this direction in the first place. Studying *ziran* got me interested in flow, and it was trying to understand the cognitive science of flow—the little there was on it at the time—that got me interested in the science of attention. Concepts from different cultures can do this for us. In the terminology of Page and Hong, concepts can act as both perspectives and heuristics. I think that we see the world through our concepts. In this sense, a new concept can give us a new perspective. And as one concept links to others, we have a new way of thinking—a new heuristic. The concept of *ziran* helps us see and think about attention and action in a new way.

The conclusion from all of this is that the concept of *ziran* gives us a fresh perspective on the paradigm of attention in cognitive science. Scientific findings consistent with the idea of *ziran* as high attention with low effort throw into doubt the traditional paradigm of attention as effort.

Chapter 4

Broadening Aesthetics

Spontaneity, the Somatic Arts, and Improvisation

Two Problems in Aesthetics

In this chapter, we move to the topic of aesthetics. The object of this chapter is simple and straightforward—to see art in a new light, in a way that will allow us to create new theories and practices. Think of the word *art,* and probably the first thing that comes to your mind is painting, maybe a Michelangelo, a Van Gogh, or a Matisse. Art under this paradigm is static and two-dimensional. Of course, there are other, more active, arts, such as musical performance, dance, and drama. Those also count as high art for most Westerners, but they are usually not the first to come to mind. The aim of this chapter is to challenge this preconception, and through the Chinese notion of *ziran,* create a new perspective on art and aesthetics—one that is dynamic and embodied, one in which fluid movement is fundamental to both the creation and the appreciation of art.

I will take the idea of *ziran* from chapter 1 and see how it can help us make progress on two problems in aesthetic theory:

1. What is the distinguishing mark of artistry?

2. What is improvisation?

The answer to both of these involves what I call *aesthetic spontaneity.* After showing how a well-defined notion of aesthetic spontaneity can help us make progress with regard to these two questions, I'll broaden the conversation through the use of an informative diagram that will help us better understand not only artistic activities but activities in general.

Let me first motivate the above two problems, and then I'll go into more detail about how to answer them. Discussing the art of Chinese calligraphy, the writer Chiang Yee says:

> An identical series of characters can be written by two hands and though the lines described are precisely the same, with no difference at all between the curves and the structures, the work of the one hand will be an object of joyful contemplation, while the work of the other appears so common that the untutored onlooker feels he could do as well himself.[1]

If you know anything at all about Chinese calligraphy, you know it is common for people who are learning it to copy the masterpieces that have come before. Figure 4.1 is a famous example from one of the celebrated calligraphers of the Northern Song Dynasty. If you were an advanced student of calligraphy, you might copy this over and over, and if you got to a really high level, you could copy it so that it looked almost identical to the original, and yet a connoisseur might look at your copy and say, "Eh, it's just not right. There's something missing." So the question is: What accounts for the gap between the masterpiece and the pretty good imitation or between a great work of original calligraphy and a merely good work of original calligraphy? That's the first question we'll try to make progress on through the concept of *ziran*.

The second question has to do with improvisation. Improvisation is a fairly robust field in contemporary philosophical aesthetics and musicology. Below are several interpretations of the notion of improvisation from recent literature:

- "In improvisational performance, the creative process is the product." (Keith Sawyer)[2]

- "An improvised performance is one in which the structural [versus expressive] properties of a performance are not completely determined by decisions made prior to the time of performance." (James Young and Carl Matheson)[3]

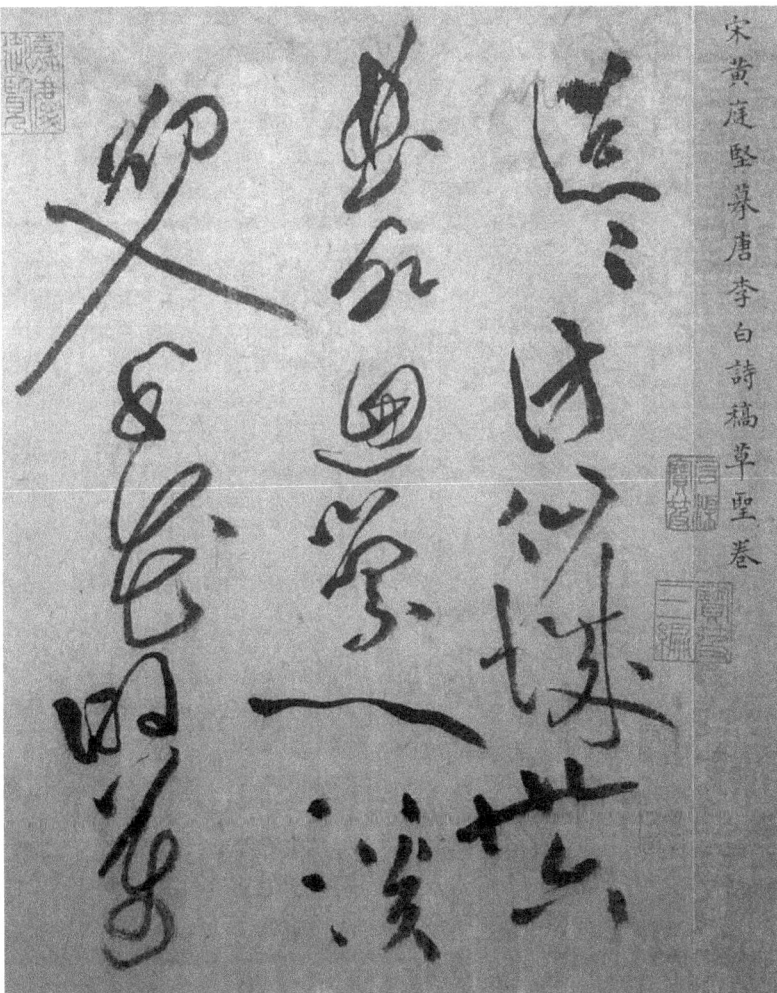

Figure 4.1. Huang Tingjian 黃庭堅, A Poem by Li Bai *Shu Li Bai shi* 書李白詩.

- "[Musical improvisation is] real-time musical decision making . . . while engaged in a performance." (Richard Cochrane)[4]
- "The realization of all aspects of a composition not precisely indicated by the musical score are improvised" (Carol Gould and Kenneth Keaton)[5]

- "Musical improvisation is the spontaneous creation of a musical work as it is being performed." (Philip Alperson)[6]

The articles from which these ideas originate focus on the topic of improvisation[7] and are quite insightful each on its own, but when you put them together and attempt to analyze what exactly improvisation is, some of the definitions of improvisation contradict one another, some overlap, and some meet up but then diverge. As a consequence, the authors often seem to be simply talking past each other. This is the second problem that we will try to make progress on through the resources of the notion of *ziran*. I will show that if we define terms precisely, especially the term *spontaneity,* which is used quite often by these authors, we can get a clearer understanding of improvisation and create a unified taxonomy that is useful to all theorists of improvisation.

Art, Nature, and Movement: The Category of Somatic Art

In this section, I shall discuss spontaneity in art broadly and then apply our new understanding to improvisation in the next section. I'd like to suggest that there is something to be learned about art and aesthetics from the notion of Daoist spontaneity,[8] so the best place to begin is the notion of art in ancient China. The earliest explicit conception of art in early China is the six arts (*liu yi* 六藝): ritual propriety (*li* 禮), music (*yue* 樂), archery (*she* 射), charioteering (*yu* 御/馭), brush writing (*shu* 書), and calculation (*shu* 數). This notion of art (*yi*) is vague but parallels English "art" in its evolution from a subject of study to a practice that produces objects of aesthetic worth. These six were the arts that any educated person of the period was expected to master. In that sense, they resemble the liberal arts of ancient Rome and Medieval times: grammar, logic, rhetoric, arithmetic, geometry, music, and astronomy. One thing that is interesting to notice about the Confucian six arts is that all of them, or almost all of them, are embodied and involve movement to an important extent. This is easily apparent in all but the sixth one, which requires a little explanation. In that period, calculation involved the following kinds of things: calendrical, military, and prognostic calculations, as well as farming, engineering, and commerce measurements. From these, it is easy to see how it might also essentially involve embodiment and movement.[9]

The earliest version of the character *yi* 藝 is from oracle bones and is written like this 埶. According to Bernard Karlgren, it is a person kneeling and planting a seedling.[10] The image of the cultivation of a seedling suggests that there is something about the idea of art that involves cultivation and development, as in a skilled movement. After the early period, *yi* retained its meaning of a skill, acquired a sense of aesthetic productivity, and lost its meaning as a subject of study for the educated class. In this transition, most of the six arts fell out of the category of art (*yi*). Ritual propriety continued prominently in the culture but was not identified as an art. Really, only music and brush writing continued as arts in their own right. Brush writing, which we refer to as *calligraphy* when it has the full aesthetic flavor of a form of art, became the paramount art form in China. This is important to understand because when we're working in cross-cultural philosophy, it is essential to try to become as aware as possible of our intuitions about certain terms. When we think of "art," maybe we think of Michelangelo or contemporary abstract painting or public art. But if we are working in the field of Chinese aesthetics and raise the subject of art, the first thing that should come to mind is calligraphy.

Chiang Yee says, "The fundamental inspiration of calligraphy, as of all the arts in China, is nature."[11] Now, what is your intuition of nature? Hopefully, by this point in the book, as we began in chapter 1 from the Chinese tradition, your intuition is not national parks and charismatic wild animals. Instead, within a Chinese context, it should be notions connected with Daoist spontaneity, especially involving movement.

Here is how Chiang describes some of the fundamental strokes that are used in constructing Chinese characters. He describes them in nature terminology. Note also that when he uses this terminology, he tends to characterize it with images of movement.[12]

- Horizontal line *heng* 橫: "so written as to seem like a formation of cloud stretching from a thousand miles away and abruptly terminating"[13]

- Dot *dian* 點: "giving the impression of a rock falling with all its force from a high cliff"[14]

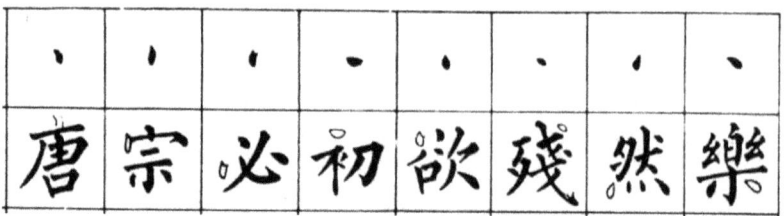

- Downward stroke *na* 捺: "made from left to right ... like a wave suddenly rolling up or a flying cloud emitting growls of thunder!"[15]

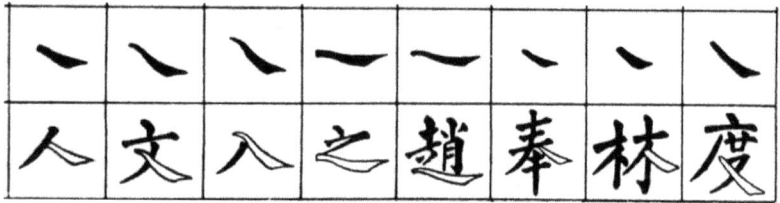

Chiang's insights show us that when we think of art in traditional China, again taking calligraphy as a model, it involves nature to a significant degree, and nature involves to a significant degree movement. Thus, we get something like this:

- Art as nature
- Art as movement
- Art ≈ Nature ≈ Movement

In other words, the concept of art should invoke associations of nature and movement, or natural movement.

If we get an understanding of Chinese art as inherently involving a sense of nature, which in turn inherently involves a sense of movement, it becomes obvious that the notion of spontaneity, as described in chapter 1, must be relevant. Spontaneity (*ziran*) is, in fact, centrally involved in both the creation and the evaluation of the arts in China. We will return to this topic shortly, but let's summarize where we are so far. By looking at the six arts in early China and how they inherently involved movement and at Chiang Yee's description of calligraphic strokes (calligraphy being the prime high art in China) in terms of natural movement, we see that movement—specifically, natural movement—is inherent in the very idea of art in Chinese aesthetics. This is consistent with our conclusions in chapter 1, in which ideal human moment was conceptualized as natural.

Now, I draw your attention first back to chapters 2 and 3, where I introduced and then discussed the notion of flow, or autotelic activity. At the risk of repeating myself, and for those who may have begun reading the book at this chapter, let me remind you of the characteristics of flow identified by Csikszentmihalyi:

- Altered sense of time
- High level of concentration
- Confidence and comfort in meeting each new high challenge
- Absence of felt effort
- Absence of self-consciousness

Hopefully, you recognize a similarity between the notion of flow as described by Csikszentmihalyi and the notion of Daoist spontaneity as described in chapter 1. I am not the only one to have noticed this similarity. Other scholars have pointed it out as well. In fact, Csikszentmihalyi himself acknowledged the similarity in his book *Flow*.[16] Just to remind you, some examples of activities where flow can be achieved are rock climbing, playing sports, performing music, and playing chess. In the literature, it's often said that being in flow can be conducive to excelling in any of these activities. Recall my friend the professional pianist (from chapter 2), who says that when he goes on stage, he hopes every time that he can be in a state of flow during the performance. Notice that of the examples I gave just now, all of them, except chess, involve significant physical movements. The association of art-as-movement and flow-as-excellence immediately shows us the relevance of flow to the artistic process. The connection of flow to art in the Chinese tradition is easily apparent—ideal movement is fluid and natural. But we don't have to confine ourselves to the Chinese tradition.

Csikszentmihalyi got started studying flow by studying artists in the United States. He wasn't studying flow originally. Originally, he was exploring what kind of experience goes into creating art, particularly painting. He was surprised when there was quite a bit of consistency in how painters characterized their experiences while creating. He then wondered if a similar experience occurs in other domains, so he started exploring other activities. The way he did this was to give his subjects a beeper and then beep them at random times throughout the day, at which time the subjects would immediately sit down and fill out a questionnaire about their subjective experience in the previous moments. He also conducted targeted interviews, and in those we see statements such as the ones we saw from rock climbers in chapter 2, which, to repeat, were:

- "You don't feel like you're doing something as a conscious being; you're adapting to the rock and becoming part of it."
- "You're so involved in what you're doing [that] you aren't thinking about yourself as separate from the immediate activity."
- "Somehow the right thing is done without you ever thinking about it or doing anything at all. . . . It just happens. And yet you're more concentrated."
- "The right decisions are made, but not rationally. Your mind is shut down and your body just goes."

One thing that is interesting about these statements is that they seem to involve what we might call unselfconsciousness, a dropping away of a sense of self, as a person is engrossed in an activity. We saw how this was important in conceptualizing a notion of action without agency in chapter 2. Here, it takes on an aesthetic significance.

Unselfconscious movement in flow activities, especially artistic flow activities, provides a bridge from art as it is conducted in contemporary times in our society to a traditional Chinese view of art as natural movement. This connection can provide us with a special insight about art—not just about traditional Chinese art but about art broadly. You may be thinking to yourself right now, "Well, wait a minute, I can think of several arts that don't have anything to do with movement per se, so what kind of insight can you really be bringing to art generally?"

Right! I'm suggesting that if you can think of some arts in which fluid movement—and the notion of spontaneity described so far—is fundamental to the creation and appreciation of the art, maybe that tells us something about *that* kind of art. Maybe we can recognize a new category of art based on this idea, and from which we can get insights about the various arts that fall under that category. I suggest that we can do this, and that we call this kind of art *somatic art,* meaning that it fundamentally involves bodily movement of the artist in both the process of creation and the process of appreciation.[17] Can the ideas we've raised so far give us insight about these kinds of art? I believe they can. Think, for example, about ballet, jazz improvisation, theatre performance, drip painting in the style of Jackson Pollock, Chinese calligraphy, and some kinds of Chinese ink wash painting. In each of these, the process of creating the art is apparent right in the art. You cannot have an evaluation or appreciation of the art without considering the movement involved in the instantiation of the piece.[18]

In a discussion of Chinese calligraphy, the scholar Lothar Ledderose, says:

> The art of calligraphy is unique among the arts of the world in that the process of creation in all its consecutive phases is visible in the object. A proper viewer follows with his eyes the brush movements through each of the characters and the sequence of the lines. He thus re-creates for himself the moments of the actual creation.[19]

Maybe Chinese calligraphy is not really so unique. I suggest that the principle Ledderose finds in Chinese calligraphy is also applicable to all of the somatic arts. We can take this idea of the creative process from China, lift it out, and apply it to a broader range of arts, such as dance, musical performance, drama, etc. In all of these, the creative process is visible in the art, and the art is evaluated in part on the basis of the natural fluidity achieved in the movement. Even in English, we sometimes praise artistic movement as "natural."[20] In a 2016 review, Alastair Macaulay praises Mark Morris' "honest, natural dancers."[21] In a 2014 review, Gia Kourlas praises "Ms. Fleet, one of the [Paul Taylor] company's most natural, fluent dancers," and says that "Mr. Taylor's definition of modern dance is . . . an extension of nature."[22]

To summarize, a somatic art is an art in which the movements of the artist are apparent in the art product and (1) the fluidity at the movement contributes to its excellence and (2) the excellence of the art is judged at least in part on the fluidity of the moment. This notion of somatic art can now give us some insight into our first question above: What is the distinguishing mark of artistry—what is the mark that sets the masterpiece off from the just-okay imitation? Perhaps it is the natural fluidity of the movement. That's insightful but still somewhat vague. Can we describe this excellence in richer detail? Chiang Yee provides us with a possible answer.

Chiang Yee says, the really good piece is "vitalized by emotional energy."[23] *Emotional energy* is a term often used in contemporary English to praise musical and dance performances. It also happens to be very close to how the Chinese traditionally answer the question of what sets off a masterwork in a traditional art. I recently posed Chiang Yee's question to some Chinese friends who engage in traditional arts, and they answered with the following terms as marks of excellence: *shen* 神, *qi* 氣, and *yun* 韻, or *qiyun* 氣韻. Chiang Yee's "vitalized by emotional energy" is a pretty good translation of these endemic Chinese terms, all of which have an ancient heritage that has to do with vitality, energy, and the work of art. In other words, they are descriptions of movement. The latter term, *qiyun,* is how Xie He 謝赫 (in the sixth century) talked about the mark of a great work of visual art. Xie was the first person in Chinese history to write a tract specifically on the aesthetics of visual art, kicking off a long tradition that has built on his ideas and still persists today.[24]

I sent Chiang Yee's quotation about identical characters by different hands to a Chinese acquaintance who is a professional calligrapher.[25] His answer to the question of what makes a great work of art was: *qi* 氣. He then volunteered a definition of *qi* as an inner rhythm (*neizai de jiezou* 內在的節奏).[26]

The authenticity of the calligraphy piece by Huang Tingjian in Figure 4.1 is actually in dispute. According to the display of it at an exhibition at the National Palace Museum, Taiwan, two connoisseurs who possessed it over the years judged that it was a copy—because "the brushwork is light and superficial *bi li qing fu* 筆力輕浮." This terminology is the opposite of "to have *qi* or *shen*." It is an evaluation of the artist's movement as evident in the ink. In the same exhibition, a piece attributed to Zhang Jizhi 張即之 of the Southern Song dynasty is also suspected of being a copy, because "the brushwork is somewhat weak *bi li shao ruo* 筆力稍弱" (Figure 4.2). In a neighboring cabinet, a piece by the Ming dynasty's Dong Qichang 董其昌, on the other hand, which is said by Dong to be based on the style of the great Eastern Jin dynasty calligraphers Wang Xizhi 王羲之 and Wang Xianzhi 王獻之, is described as "stunning in its energetic rhythm *miao de shen yun* 妙得神韻" (see Figure 4.3). Dong, though merely copying the style of predecessors, has clearly, according to this critic, succeeded in expressing the energy and vitality of the original.

I'd like to suggest that these Chinese attempts to identify the distinguishing mark of artistry (or its lack) are consistent with what I've said about Daoist spontaneity and autotelicity. To bring this idea

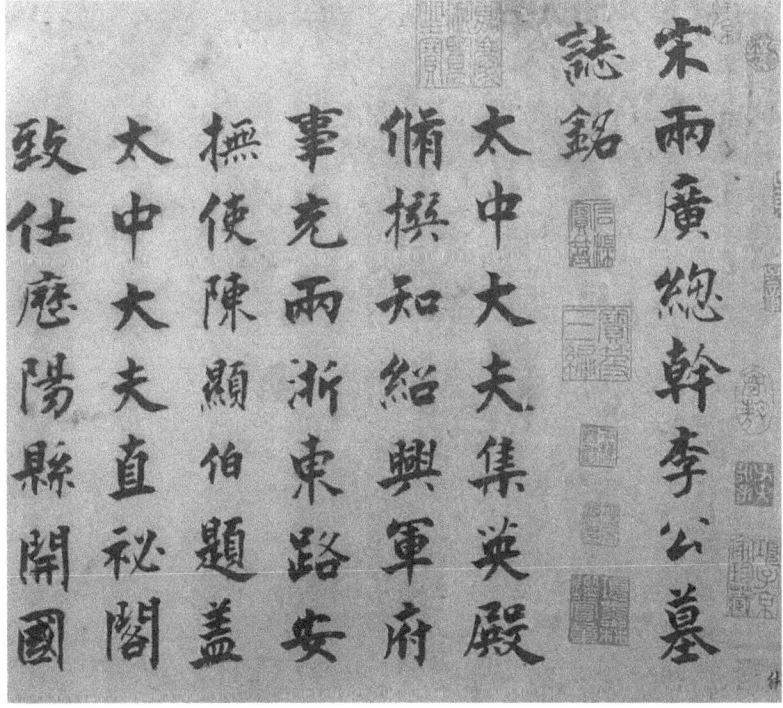

Figure 4.2. Zhang Jizhi, Li Kan Memorial Inscription *Shu Li Kan mu zhi ming* 書李衎墓志銘.

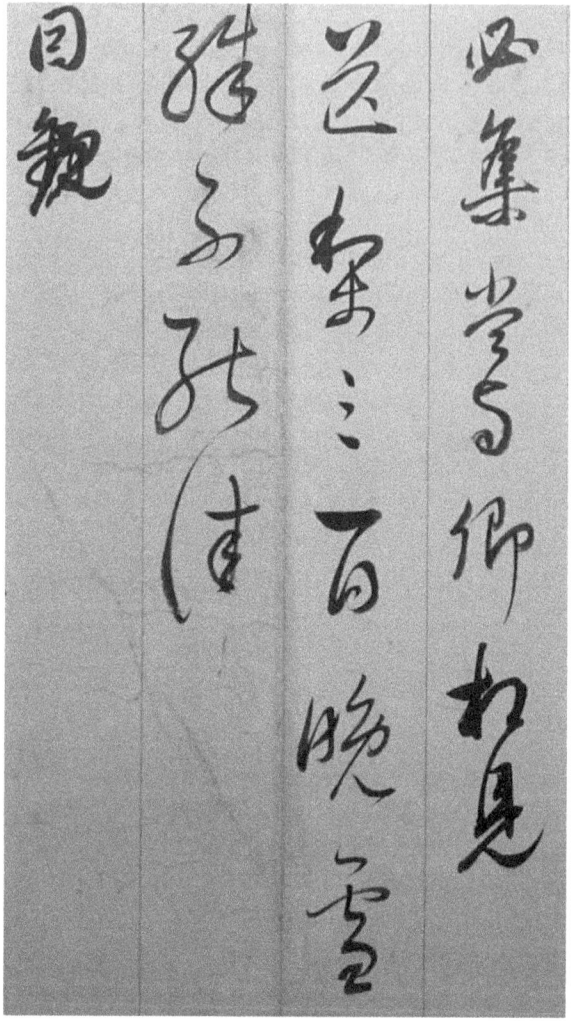

Figure 4.3. Dong Qichang, From a Jin Copybook *Jie lin Jin tie* 節臨晉帖.

into the present, we can refer to it as *aesthetic spontaneity*. The great artist, in the process of performing art is (consciously or not) working from aesthetic spontaneity—a highly cultivated Daoist spontaneity, or *ziran*. Following the definition of *ziran* from chapter 1, the artist who achieves, or expresses, aesthetic spontaneity has a high level of attention and a concentration, or collection, of other cognitive-affective aspects relevant to the particular domain of activity. The artist has let go of distractions and other concerns outside of that domain of activity, including self-consciousness itself. The artist is sensitive and responsive to the subtle cues of the activity. And the artist's movements both look and feel at ease.[27]

Let's be clear that we have narrowed the applicable range of art down to the somatic arts. And we have said that the distinguishing mark of artistry in the somatic arts is aesthetic spontaneity. Such an idea is rare but not unknown in the West. According to the artist Lee Krasner, the influential modern painting instructor Hans Hofmann once stopped by to visit Jackson Pollock and view his work. Hofmann said, "You are very talented; you should join my class. But you do not work from nature." To which Pollock replied: "I *am* nature."[28] Considering the discussion above of nature as fluid, spontaneous movement, Pollack's remark makes sense. When Pollack executed his drip painting, in an artistic process that took him years to perfect, maybe what marks it as great is this kind of spontaneity—that he is able to achieve aesthetic spontaneity as he creates the art, aesthetic spontaneity being: concentration, letting go, responsiveness, and ease.

Now if we want to study the somatic arts further, we have some concrete characteristics that we can analyze and explore. They describe the theory behind expressive terms such as *shen, qi,* and *yun*. We can use the theoretical terms to think more about the process of critiquing and evaluating art. We can also think about whether any of the capacities of aesthetic spontaneity are able to be cultivated in an artist. If we want achieve aesthetic spontaneity, which might be most tractable to adjustment and cultivation? Which are more essential to evaluating somatic art?

Recall again my pianist friend who wants to achieve flow each time he goes on stage. He asked me how to be able to achieve it each time. Maybe the process of cultivation of flow can be explored through the interpretation of aesthetic spontaneity given here. The Daoist concept of *ziran* helps us see that there is a distinct category of art that we can call somatic art, which broadens our aesthetics in a valuable way. There is much more to explore in this new field.

Improvisation and Aesthetic Spontaneity

Let me pause and remind you what I'm trying to do. I'm trying to lift an idea out of traditional Chinese philosophy and put it into a language that is useful for us today so that we can see some insights about things that we think about anyway and maybe make some progress in that field. Now I will move from the topic of the somatic arts generally to the more specific topic of improvisation within the somatic arts, applying the notion of *ziran* to artistic improvisation.

Recall for a moment the contrasting senses of improvisation raised at the beginning of this chapter. The problem I see in these treatments of improvisation is that in ten core articles on improvisation,[29] there are no fewer than seven distinct understandings of improvisation, which suggests that the authors, instead of having a conversation about a single topic, are discussion a variety of rival concepts that are difficult to unify. The term most often associated with "improvisation" in the articles in question is *creativity*, followed by the terms *spontaneity, interpretation, fluency, extemporaneous, deliberate, convention, performance,* and *composition*. Other relevant terms in the articles are: *impromptu, authenticity,* and *individuality*. Almost never, with the exception of "improvisation," are any of the terms above defined by the authors. The authors assume that the reader knows exactly what they are talking about when they use terms such as *spontaneity* or *impromptu* or *convention*. Looking carefully at the articles, however, one sees that this failure to define terms makes it impossible to analyze the concept of improvisation across the articles.

These authors discuss the topic of improvisation across a variety of fields, which accounts partly for the divergences. For example, when Keith Sawyer (see Table 4.1) discusses improvisation, he begins with Picasso—probably not the first person to come to mind for you in the context of improvisation. Sawyer refers specifically to a documentary film that shows Picasso in the process of painting, where he is facing a blank canvass and begins by drawing a line of a female figure. As he draws, Picasso is reminded of a matador's leg. He then paints over the female figure and paints a bullfighting scene. Somehow that reminds him of the seashore, so he paints over the bullfighting scene, and paints the seashore, and so on. This, according to Sawyer, is a kind of improvisation. It is also a process of composition, and Sawyer takes composition as an essential feature of improvisation.[30] In Table 4.1, I summarize the key perspectives of some of the articles in question and add, in bold, a description of that kind of improvisation in my own terminology that is consistent with what the particular author's theory.

Table 4.1. Summary of Main Perspectives on Improvisation

Sawyer	public, ephemeral, collective performance; the process is the product; Picasso as improviser—**compositional**
Young & Matheson	indeterminacy of structural properties—**substitutive, elaborative, completive**
Cochrane	constants and variables in a musical performance—**derivative**
Gould & Keaton	any variation in a musical performance; conceptually independent of impromptu performance; all musical performance requires improvisation—**interpretive**
Day	ordinary, unrehearsed activity—**compositional**
Brown	carved out as it is being played; situation, forced, no script—**compositional**
Gilmour	improvisation away from convention—**inventive**
Carter	produces new paradigms—**inventive**
Sterritt	**authenticity, spontaneity, individuality**

James Young and Carl Matheson discuss the indeterminacy of structural properties, mostly in the context of jazz performance. In jazz, you sometimes have a score and sometimes not (as in free jazz). Sometimes you pop out a part of the score and add your own creative substitution. Sometimes you elaborate on the score that's there. And sometimes you complete an incomplete score. Some of this is applicable not just to jazz but to other forms of musical performance and performance art as well. These kinds of improvisation can be called *substitutive*, *elaborative*, and *completive*, respectively. Just like we can label Sawyer's notion of improvisation as compositional, we can also apply labels to Young and Matheson's notion of improvisation: in this case using three labels for three distinct kinds of improvisation. Already, then, we have not just improvisation as a vague term but four distinct kinds of improvisation.

Richard Cochrane discusses improvisation in terms of musical performance always involving constants and variables (even in free jazz). His angle on it is that a musical performance always starts from somewhere and always has some constraints and so is fundamentally derivative. This is notably different from Sawyer's view of improvisation as compositional. Now, we have a fifth kind of improvisation: *derivative*.

Carol Gould and Kenneth Keaton discuss improvisation in the context of classical music performance. Their main claim is that jazz is not the only musical form that is heavy on improvisation. Classical music, they argue, necessarily involves improvisation. Like Cochrane, they say that any variation in a musical performance counts as improvisation, and so in that sense all music performance requires it. Not everything about a musical performance, they say, can be incorporated into a score. A successful performance always depends on how a musician improvises the unwritten aspects of a score. Further, improvisation in this sense can occur prior to the performance itself, in the process of preparation, and not just in the live performance. This, also, is a kind of derivative improvisation, but derivative in the sense of being *interpretive*—our sixth label for kinds of improvisation.

William Day[31] sees improvisation in music as akin to improvisation across a very broad range of activities, such as day-to-day conversation. We don't plan out an informal chat ahead of time and write it down in a script. Instead, it comes to us as the conversation unfolds. For our purposes, we can class everyday improvisation as *compositional*, like Sawyer's notion above.[32]

Lee Brown[33] discusses improvisation in the context of free jazz, saying that a piece is "carved out as it is being played."[34] He specifies that a free jazz performance, as improvisation, is situated, meaning that it occurs in a particular time and particular place. Further, it is forced, meaning that it is not open to revision—you cannot go back and make changes. Once a note is played, that's it. He also emphasizes that it is unscripted. All of these terms—situated, impromptu, and unscripted—can describe this kind of improvisation, but fundamentally they fall under the label of *compositional*, as with Day and Sawyer above.

Like Sawyer, John Gilmour[35] discusses improvisation in painting, but instead of Picasso, he focuses on Cézanne and other impressionists. According to Gilmour, these painters are working from nature, but they are also being inventive. They are improvising away from convention—in two senses. Gilmour says that Cézanne, in his late landscapes, no longer sees landscapes in the conventional sense and that his new way of seeing is depicted through the new color schemes that he uses in his paintings. The second sense in which Gilmour says that Cézanne improvises on convention is in formal technique, such as his brushwork. In fact, the change in color schemes can represent both of these kinds of invention in that they both offer a new way of seeing color and they afford a new technique for representing distance. Gilmour does not name this kind of improvisation from convention. Due to its fundamental inventiveness, I call it *inventive* improvisation. It is our seventh kind of improvisation.

In an extensive discussion of improvisation in dance, Curtis Carter[36] goes even farther into the idea of improvisation as the development of new paradigms, a conception of improvisation that is also *inventive*.

David Sterritt[37] says that successful improvisation tells you something about the person who is improvising, that a kind of authenticity comes through. He refers to this kind of improvisation as involving spontaneity and individuality. You can probably see how this idea of spontaneity in improvisation might be relevant to the kind of spontaneity discussed in previous chapters. We'll get back to this distinct kind of improvisation momentarily, but having raised the topic of spontaneity, an essential preparatory step to getting clear about the kinds of improvisation requires getting clear about the important descriptive vocabulary of improvisation associated with spontaneity in Sterritt's sense.

The word *spontaneous* occurs over and over in these articles, without anyone pausing to define it. Context can go some way in pinpointing the meaning of the author. Sometimes spontaneous means impromptu, sometimes unscripted, and sometimes it means something similar to what I've described so far as aesthetic spontaneity. I'd like to suggest, as a way to clarify things, that when we use the word *spontaneous* in the context of improvisation, we don't use it with the meaning of impromptu. If we mean impromptu (i.e., without preparation), we say, "impromptu." That makes it perfectly clear. If we mean unscripted, we say, "unscripted," not "spontaneous." By *spontaneous*, from here on out, we shall mean only *aesthetic spontaneity* as defined above (i.e., concentrating, letting go, responsiveness, and ease). It would be very unlikely for these authors to mean exactly what I mean by aesthetic spontaneity, as it is derived from the Daoist tradition, so let's set further discussion of this issue aside for the moment and clarify other terms first, as follows:

- Impromptu—unrehearsed, unscheduled
- Unscripted—not written down, not formulated in detail ahead of time
- Inventive—novel, straying from convention
- Convention—preestablished ways of doing something, agreed explicitly or implicitly within a group
- Interpretive—executed outside of instructions
- Completive—filling gaps
- Elaborative—adding to an existing score or script
- Substitutive—replacing part(s) of an existing score or script

With this key improvisational terminology clarified, along with the seven labels of improvisation established above, we can create a detailed, nuanced taxonomy of "improvisation" that covers all the ground that is covered in the articles in question, and with only a smidgeon of contradiction. In Table 4.2, I lay out the seven labels of improvisation using the newly clarified vocabulary.

Organizing these seven labels of improvisation is not just a matter of listing them. Because the seven labels for improvisation are culled from very diverse articles, they don't easily align. Instead, there is some overlap and even contradiction. The main hurdle here is that some scholars (Sawyer, Gilmour, Day, and Brown) see improvisation as importantly compositional, while others (Young, Matheson, Cochrane, Gould, Keaton, Carter) see improvisation as fundamentally derivative. This presents a hurdle for the systematizer because these two views of improvisation are potentially contradictory. If you view improvisation as mainly compositional, then improvisation as mere interpretation or elaboration may not count as improvisation at all.[38] The way to get over this hurdle is to acknowledge the conflict but not to view the two as mutually exclusive. There can be both compositional and derivative improvisation.

To do this, we formulate two basic classes of improvisation: (1) wholesale composition and (2) derivative improvisation (improvising from a score or a script).[39] They are labeled A and B in the table.

Table 4.2. Classes and Kinds of Improvisation

A. Wholesale Composition	B. Derivative Improvisation
1. Compositional Improvisation. Ex.: Picasso painting, improvisational theater, free jazz.	1. Inventive Improvisation. Ex.: Cézanne painting, contemporary adaptation of Shakespeare.
	2. Interpretive Improvisation. Ex.: Classical piano performance, classical violin performance.
	3. Completive Improvisation. Ex.: Cadenza in classical music.
	4. Elaborative Improvisation. Ex.: Small ensemble jazz improvisation.
	5. Substitutive Improvisation. Ex.: Small ensemble jazz improvisation.

Wholesale creation is creating something from (almost) nothing.[40] This is compositional improvisation—working from a blank canvas or score, unscripted and unplanned, perhaps involving play or exploration. This is Sawyer's Picasso and labeled A1 in the table. Sawyer calls it creative improvisation, associating it with problem finding, as opposed to problem solving. His emphasis is on the process, not the product. Other obvious examples of compositional improvisation would be improvisational theater and free jazz.

The class of derivative improvisation is more varied, with five distinct kinds of improvisation. The first is inventive improvisation (B1), the kind discussed above as improvising from convention. It is exemplified in the new techniques used by Impressionist painters. Another example would be an adaptation of Shakespeare's *Romeo and Juliet* set in a contemporary context.

Classical music (following Gould and Keaton) would be a prime example of interpretive improvisation (B2), in which the score is as complete as it gets but does not fully capture the potential for the expressive properties of a performance.

Also from classical music, a cadenza is an intentionally unscripted part of an otherwise complete musical score. The score is the basis, and the performer improvises from the structure and style of the score to complete it through improvising the cadenza. This is completive improvisation (B3).

Jazz improvisation often takes a complete score as its basis and improvises from that. If the musicians elaborate on it, that is elaborative improvisation (B4). If they subtract from it and then add their own creative portions, that is substitutive improvisation (B5).[41]

From the above taxonomy, we see that our seven labels for seven putatively different kinds of improvisation turns out to actually involve two classes of improvisation and six kinds—one kind of compositional improvisation and five kinds of derivative improvisation. This taxonomy of improvisation is useful for bringing different conceptions of improvisation together from a variety of pursuits, creating a harmony of the many definitions that are out there.[42] By defining each term clearly and setting the vague term *spontaneity* aside, we see how each kind of improvisation can stand alone as distinct—not as the only exclusive definition of improvisation but as one variety among others. Following this taxonomy, we should be wary of referring to improvisation as such and instead refer to the particular kind of improvisation that is meant in the particular context. Does jazz music involve improvisation? The question is too vague. Which kind of jazz are you talking about? Free jazz involves compositional improvisation. Does a jazz standard also involve compositional improvisation? No, it involves derivative improvisation—elaborative, substitutive, or completive, or some combination. Can painting also be improvisational? Yes, but not in exactly the same way as music. Painting can be simultaneously compositional and derivative. And what about classical music? That can also be improvisational, but largely in an interpretive sense, sometimes in a completive sense.

There is more to be said about this taxonomy. I intend it as a starting point for a larger, more detailed discussion about the classes and kinds of improvisation. No longer should we refer to improvisation as just one thing. For example, what about other endeavors and activities not discussed by the above articles, such as woodworking or sports or conceptual art? Surely there is improvisation involved, but what kind(s)? The Action diagram in the following section might help answer this question.

Where does all this leave the spontaneity of improvisation? Jack Kerouac is famous for writing in a stream of consciousness style.

Physically, his writing was so dynamic that it might not be a stretch to characterize it as somatic.[43] Further, Kerouac said that when he wrote, it was important that he went into a kind of trance. I interpret that as a kind of unselfconsciousness. In Sterritt's discussion of improvisation, he takes Kerouac's writing as a prime example. Kerouac said that when you get out of yourself, that is when your true self[44] comes to the fore and is expressed in your art. Sterritt refers to this state of consciousness as *spontaneity*. This sense of spontaneity is in the background of several of these articles and is prominent in Sterritt's. Improvisation, on this interpretation, reveals the true self.[45] Not coincidentally, when you look back at traditional Chinese art, *ziran*—aesthetic spontaneity—is also understood as revealing the true self, from both Confucian and Daoist perspectives.

When that acquaintance of mine who is a professional calligrapher explained his idea of the distinguishing mark of a great work, he went on to give an example, elaborating on his use of the term *qi* 氣. He said, suppose there are twins who are identical in appearance, but one of them is educated and the other is not. He said that the *qizhi* 氣質 (character) of the educated one will shine through even though the two are in all other ways identical in appearance. This idea of one's character shining through is consistent with the notion of spontaneity being revelatory of the true self. Clement Greenberg, art critic during the era of the American Abstract Expressionists, said of Jackson Pollock, "If he was anything, he was true."[46]

Perhaps improvisation gets us to the purest form of aesthetic spontaneity in the somatic arts. Perhaps, through improvisation, we can, as if gazing through a window, see into the sincere artistic intentions (or nonintentions) of the artist as the creative process unfolds. This conclusion is admittedly tentative and deserves further exploration. The subject is complicated by the fact that some artists have rather dark sides to their personalities, and one wonders what it really means to see their true selves in their art.

Form and Syntax: The Action Diagram

To summarize where we have come so far, I raised two problems at the beginning of the chapter. The first was the distinguishing mark of artistry, and what we were able to find is that we can distinguish a specific kind of art, called somatic art, and that the distinguishing mark in the somatic arts is aesthetic spontaneity—understood specifically as implying nature-as-movement, constituted by concentration, letting go (including of self-consciousness), responsiveness, and ease. That was step one. By being clear about these four aspects of aesthetic spontaneity and then clarifying the definitions of allied terms, in step two we get a clearer understanding of improvisation itself. We were able to distinguish it into two classes and six kinds, in all of which, we can speculate, aesthetic spontaneity reveals the true self.

I've discussed above that whereas Aristotle favors a theory of action that crosses all domains of activity, Zhuangzi prefers to discuss optimal action within a single domain of activity. This latter conception of activity has certain advantages. When we act, we often do so within a specific set of limits and parameters. Consider the game of chess. To play the game, one has to accept the rules that make up the game. To play outside the rules is to stop playing the game altogether. To move the rook, for example, you can move only in two stipulated ways. If you move the rook in some way other than horizontally or vertically, you are no longer playing chess. This kind of rule is constitutive. Constitutive rules make the activity what it is. By contrast, violating traffic laws while driving invites a penalty. This kind of rule is regulative. Regulative rules regulate the actions of the activity.[47] Constitutive and regulative rules are syntactic constraints, or rules of syntax.

In classical ballet, there are certain conventions about particular kinds of movements, such as the sauté (a jump with legs apart and toes pointed down) or the numbered positions of the arms and feet (number one of the feet, for example, has the heels together with the toes pointing in opposition directions, left and right). These *forms,* or *formal* movements, can be qualitatively better or worse according to standard conventions, but they are neither constitutive nor regulative. Doing a pirouette doesn't necessarily make your activity a classical ballet dance, and failing to do one perfectly doesn't bring a dance performance to a halt or invite official censure.

Some activities have more (or more complex) rules of syntax. Playing chess, for example, is more complicated than playing "go fish." Doing the full 108 forms of Yang style taiji is more complicated than the basic movements of a waltz. Likewise, some activities have more (and stricter) formal movements than others. The formal conventions of classical ballet are more strict than the conventions of modern dance, for example. And some activities, such as taiji, require a significant level of both form and syntax, while other activities, eating a grape for example, have next to none.

We can combine the form and syntax spectra into a phase-space diagram, with the y-axis as the number of forms or strictness of formality of individual movements within an activity and the x-axis as the amount or complexity of syntax within the same activity. Any activity can then be plotted by its degree of form and syntax (see Figure 4.4).

Eating a grape has next to no form or syntax, but it does have a little of both. Holding a grape between thumb and forefinger, for example, is more efficient than between pinky and forefinger. This would count as a formal constraint. Being situated in an upright position in order to swallow, on the other hand, is a merely practical constraint. I suggest that this kind of practical formal constraint does not count as formal constraint for the purposes of this diagram. Let us think about techniques that allow for optimal performance of an activity (such as grape between forefinger and thumb or the way a baseball player holds a bat or the way a basketball player shoots a ball) and about movements that by convention are considered aesthetically laudatory. Technical and aesthetic formal constraints are what should be plotted in the Action diagram, not mere practical constraints.

Although there are also practical syntactic constraints, such as moving the grape from a lower position to a higher position as it goes into the mouth, this is not a constitutive or regulative rule. So, similarly, we should consider constitutive, regulative, and aesthetic constraints to be the criteria for plotting an activity's syntax, not practical syntactic constraints.

Entertaining friends at a dinner party involves little to no formal constraints but does require some minor syntax—when to send out invitations, to open the door, to serve the dishes, to move from person to person conversationally, and so on. Making art is often quite the opposite, involving certain formal movements, such as how to hold the brush when painting, or a blade when sculpting clay, whereas the creation can unfold in a unique way each time. Requiring a moderate amount of form and a high amount of syntax is the activity of driving, where one's hands and feet cannot move about freely and one must follow the rules of the road.

Acrobatics, martial arts, and choreographed dances all require highly formalized movements but vary in their level of syntax. Playful

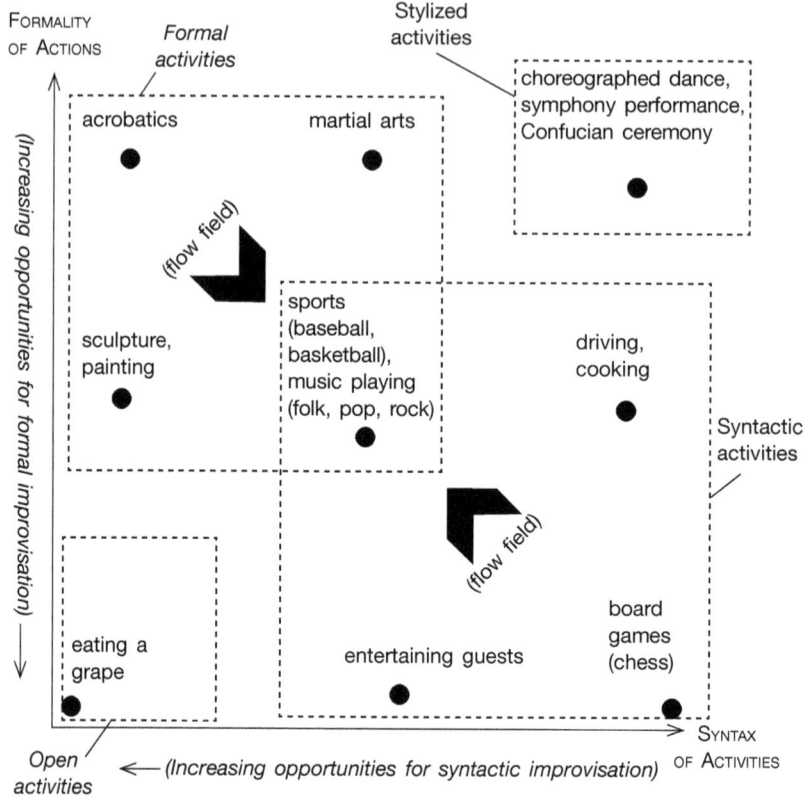

Figure 4.4. Action Diagram with axes of form and syntax.

acrobatics in an open area can be done with little to no syntax. In many martial arts, there is a responsiveness required in a sparring match that allows for a high degree of flexibility as one move or strike follows from the previous one, but fighting strategy and the give and take of strikes and blocks also provide syntactic constraints. On the far end of the axes of both syntactic and formal constraints, in the top right of the diagram, lie such activities as fully choreographed dances, symphonic performances, and some kinds of ceremonies, such as Confucian ceremonies and Catholic masses.

We have covered the perimeter of the diagram, from activities of low to high syntax but little formality (eating a grape to entertaining guests to playing a board game like chess), from low formality to high formality with little syntax (eating a grape to doing art to playfully doing acrobatics), from low to high syntax with a high level of formality (acrobatics to martial arts to choreographed dance), and from low to high formality with high syntax (chess to driving to choreographed dance). We can call activities with both low formality and low syntax *open activities*; activities with low form and moderate to high syntax *syntactic activities*; activities with low syntax and moderate to high form *formal activities*; and activities with high formality and syntax *stylized activities*.

We have left one region of the chart unmentioned so far—the center, where there is a moderate amount of both form and syntax. Here, we find sports, popular music playing (folk, pop, rock), hobbies, and crafts (woodworking, sewing). There is something to be said about this area of the diagram with respect to flow. Flow activities are high attentional activities. What is the participant paying attention to in these activities? Before you can get into flow, you must first master the basic formal and syntactic requirements of an activity. In baseball, you learn the formal movements of how to hold a bat, throw a ball, catch a fly ball, slide into a base, and so on. You also learn the rules, such as how innings progress, how runners round the bases, how to make an out, how to score a run, and so on. The formality and syntax of baseball are easy enough that anyone can learn them quickly and difficult enough to require sustained attention over long periods for true mastery. As such, they are, in my opinion, the sweet spot for achieving flow. Too easy, and you lose interest; too hard and you fatigue quickly. Not enough movement, and you feel restless; too much formal movement, and you feel frustrated. Not enough syntax, and you feel at sea; too much syntax, and you feel confused. With just enough of both, you can lose yourself in the activity, as it engages both mind and body. The *flow field*, I suggest, spreads toward the center from the syntactic activities at bottom-right and from the formal activities at top-left in such a way that the possibility of achieving flow increases for the average person as one approaches the center of the diagram. Both a lack and an excess of form or syntax require too much for most people to manage. Most people will gravitate toward the center of the diagram and diverge to the top-left or bottom-right perhaps depending on personality, talent, and other individual predilections.

The action diagram, with axes of formality and syntax, is also a convenient tool for visualizing the gradients of improvisation. Stylized activities are those with more instructions, and as one proceeds horizontally on a line toward the left, the instructions decrease and more opportunity for improvisation arises. For stylized activities, there are opportunities only for interpretive improvisation, but as one proceeds from right to left, opportunities arise for elaborative, then completive, then substitutive, and finally, at the far left, for compositional improvisation. The different kinds of jazz performance would fall somewhere in a square among the formal activities, with swing style closer to the right, moving horizontally through bebop to the left and finally to free jazz on the far left. There may also be a slight vertical drop, but not to the point of the arts at the middle left.

Proceeding horizontally in this way from fewer opportunities for improvisation to more reveals a category we may call *syntactic improvisation*. To proceed only on this axis, however, neglects *formal improvisation*, which proceeds in increasing opportunity vertically, from top to bottom in the revision of the formality of actions.

Considering the entire graph through the evolution of one kind of activity, we could look at classical ballet as an example. A fully scored, fully traditional classical ballet would fall under stylized activities at the top right, where there is opportunity only for interpretive improvisation. If one were to begin considering less completely choreographed ballets (e.g., *Giselle*), one would begin to see more opportunities arise for improvisation moving horizontally across the top of the graph. If one were to consider ballet's transition to modern dance, one would move vertically down the right side of the diagram. And if one were to consider both together, moving in the direction of dance in improvisational theater, one would move diagonally from top right to bottom left.

The notion of formal improvisation exposes the limits of the action diagram. Formal improvisation is a kind of inventive improvisation that occurs diachronically—that is, it can occur in interrupted sessions rather than over a single time-course (synchronically). For example, a choreographer who in composing a piece on a practice stage alters a traditional step, which will find its way into the performance. But this also reveals the relative broad scope of the diagram which includes not only somatic arts but goes beyond them to any activity that involves a bounded time course and requires sustained attention. To the extent that the action diagram helps us visualize the parameters of aesthetic spontaneity, flow, and improvisation, it suggests that they are relevant only to activities that are undertaken synchronically. They are relevant to diachronic activities only if such activities have long enough individual time spans to be consummated in synchronic stages. Should we create yet another technical term and call all synchronic activities that cluster in and around the flow field *flow-apt activities*?

Cultivation of Aesthetic Spontaneity

Whenever I speak about the concept of effortlessness, especially to a Chinese audience, there is often a member of the audience who says something like, "Yes, but achieving a state of effortlessness requires a great amount of effort." This is true. To the extent that effortlessness (or flow or aesthetic spontaneity) involves a skill, it requires a period of building that skill. How much effort goes into building a skill depends on one's definition of "effort" and on the participant's levels of interest and dedication. The topic of effort deserves more study, but here we will focus on the *building* part and set aside how effortful it might be.

There is a large literature in psychology, neuroscience, and kinesiology on the topic of skill building, and I won't rehearse it here, since the cultivation of aesthetic spontaneity goes beyond mere skill building. Instead, I will focus on the four aspects of Daoist spontaneity identified in chapter 1 and use the stories from Zhuangzi as a springboard for taking a first step to speculate about how aesthetic spontaneity might be cultivated. This section is necessarily preliminary and so merely suggestive. I hope that the reader can gain a few insights from it and that future scholars can take these ideas further into the realms of empirical science and formal education.

Concentration

You will recall from chapter 1 that "concentration" refers primarily to the concentration of attention. In the *Zhuangzi*, it includes the concentration, or collection, of a broader, but unspecified, range of psychic energies than just attention. In English, we also have the customary locutions, for example, of "being calm and collected" and "to collect one's wits." *Concentration* is thus a high state of attention within a particular domain of activity along with the collection and focusing of whatever other subjective or objective psychic factors may also contribute, such as a feeling of having energy, actually having more energy, being aware of cues and opportunities for action, a feeling of openness to such cues and opportunities, a feeling of confidence in the ability to meet such opportunities, and so on.

In Zhuangzi's story of the cicada catcher, the man prepares by practicing hand-eye coordination and focusing his attention to the point that the only thing he can see are the wings of the cicada. In the story of Qing the bell stand maker, he practices a kind of meditation over the course of a week, in which he concentrates his *qi* and calms his mind. As a result, when he goes into the forest to select the most appropriate tree, he is able to see attributes of the trees most relevant to the finished wood constructions.

These stories suggest that to cultivate aesthetic spontaneity beyond mere skill building, one can practice concentration within the particular domain of activity itself and beyond that can also meditate in what appears to be a cross-domain way. One of the major questions that subtends the project of cultivation of aesthetic spontaneity is whether the progress that grows out of the practices will necessarily be confined to a single domain or whether progress can be achieved across different domains of activity. Think of how practicing swinging a baseball bat will be helpful to the formal movements of batting but not helpful, and perhaps even detrimental, to learning the formal movements of swinging a golf club. Strength or flexibility training, on the other hand, might be helpful to the effectiveness of both the baseball and the golf swing. Intuitively, it seems that meditation should have cross-domain benefits. If so, the question then becomes: What kind of meditation should one do? And what about the other aspects of concentration—can those be cultivated also? The conceptual resources above help us begin to ask useful questions like these.

Letting Go

Letting go is the flip side of concentration. As you concentrate on one domain of activity, all other concerns should fall away. The cicada catcher says that despite the expansiveness of the world and the multitude of things in it, the only thing he sees is the cicada's wings. Not wavering, he would not exchange anything in the world for the wings of the cicada. The bell-stand maker, through the slow process of days-long meditation, forgets the possibilities of remuneration for his finished work, forgets that he even has a special skill, forgets that he has a body at all, even loses a sense of the boundaries around things, seeing directly, he says, into their very nature. As discussed above, the key to achieving flow, in my opinion, is the ability to lose consciousness of oneself as part of the activity, to lose any sense that "I" have anything to gain from or contribute to the activity. Instead, focus is on each opportunity for action and meeting that opportunity appropriately as it arises. The subjective feeling, rather than *I am doing it*, is *it is just happening*. We can see a loss of self-consciousness in the bell stand maker's losing a sense of his own body and skill. The cicada catcher even says he becomes in his loss of self-consciousness like a tree stump (more specifically, like a tree stump that has lost awareness).[48] In a passage in *Zhuangzi* chapter 2 that appears to be a direct reference to meditation, the mind in such a state is referred to as being like dead ash—that is, like a fire that has been put out, even though the person is clearly awake and conscious.

Responsiveness

Of the four characteristics of aesthetic spontaneity under discussion, responsiveness seems to be the most closely related to skill learning. As one learns a skill, one learns to recognize increasingly subtle cues and respond to them in increasingly subtle and accurate ways. For example, a skilled baseball player can see the rotation of the ball as it leaves the pitcher's hand. A skilled tennis player can infer the trajectory of the ball from the body movements of the opponent, swing direction of the racket, and sound of the ball coming off the racket. When Zhuangzi's bell stand maker finally goes into the forest looking for timber, he says that he is able to "match nature with nature."[49] A swimmer in roiling water in the same chapter says that he follows the eddies in and the swells out.

No doubt, there is a relationship between the cognitive-affective attainments of concentration and letting go and of responsiveness. Concentrating on a domain of activity makes one aware of the cues that may arise. Being free of distractions improves both perceptual acuity and the efficiency of action. In chapter 3, for example, we saw in Wulf's studies how invoking the self in an activity might hinder the efficiency of the movement. But whereas concentration and letting go are the psychological attributes of aesthetic spontaneity, responsiveness is in the action itself. It is where art and achievement become manifest and by which the somatic arts are in part judged.

In Western action theory, action is generally understood as beginning from a mental thrust—an act of will, prior to which no particular thing, person, or event plays a necessarily pivotal role. That's not to say that ethical action is not a response to a particular situation but that the pathway of reasoning and determination takes one well beyond the particulars to more general concerns. And as far as the notion of spontaneity goes in the West, when it is used in reference to human freedom, it is meant as freedom from all constraints of momentary conditions. This, again, shows how action theory in the West prefers, and even assumes, cross-domain applicability. In aesthetic spontaneity, by contrast, the bounds of the domain of activity determine the bounds of the available actions. Responsiveness is the ability to act swiftly in the most appropriate way to each condition as it arises within the syntax of a domain. And responsiveness is dependent in part on sensitivity. Without first being sensitive, one cannot be responsive.

One way to think of aesthetic spontaneity is to see it as more restricted than spontaneity-as-free-will. With free will, anything (within the bounds of natural law) is possible, whereas with aesthetic spontaneity, the theory applies to one domain of action at a time. However, if we compare sensitivity and responsiveness with the notion of stimulus and response in traditional experimental psychology, aesthetic spontaneity is more expansive. In behaviorist psychology, the notion of stimulus and response refers to a restricted range of behavior that is learned in association with a specific cue or set of cues. The classic example is Pavlov's dogs, which learned to drool to the sound of a metronome, with no food nearby. This process is called conditioning and is often discussed in terms that seem mechanical and impersonal. It reflects a determinist view of physics transferred to human psychology.

As a model for human behavior, sensitivity-and-responsiveness suggests, instead, a range of possible associations to a range of possible cues, with room for creative application. The word *feel* in English (as in, "I feel that it is the right thing to do") suggests something more flexible than either a stimulus-response determinism or a rule-following rationality. In traditional Chinese, from which I am drawing the idea of sensitivity and responsiveness, the operative term is *ganying* 感應, which means to feel and then respond. It is a term that refers not just to human beings but even to nature more broadly—a conception of the functioning of orderly and bountiful nature. In this way, sensitivity and responsiveness is an idea that is distinct from determinist conditioning, rule-following rationality, and anything-goes freedom. Like conditioning, it is associative; like rationality, it makes sense and leads to optimal responses; and like anything-goes freedom, it allows for creativity. But it is more flexible than conditioning and strict rationality, and it is more restricted and grounded than anything-goes freedom.

In terms of cultivation of responsiveness, the above discussion points us in the direction of not only honing appropriately manifested actions but even more importantly of grooming one's sensitivity to subtle cues. This can be achieved, of course, by practicing within a specific domain, and even breaking down the domain into subdomains, as often occurs in sports drills. One wonders if it can also be enhanced through a cross-domain practice, such as meditation (sensitizing general awareness) or hatha yoga (sensitizing general body perception).

Ease

Ease refers to both the quality of an action that appears from the outside to be performed without strain and to the subjective feeling of an action as actually being performed without a feeling of strain. This notion is different from the distinction made in chapter 3 between objective and subjective effort. Here, it is a distinction between the appearance from an observer's point of view and the feeling from an agent's first-person point of view. We'll concern ourselves specifically with the first-person feeling of ease and assume (1) that it is always conveyed successfully to observers, and (2) that the appearance of ease from an observer's point of view implies a feeling of ease from the first-person point of view.

In the story of the cicada catcher, he is described from an observer's point of view to be able to catch cicadas with his pole as easily as if he were snatching them up with his hand. He says himself that he doesn't waver and then exclaims, "How could I not get it?" expressing what appears to be a feeling of confidence and ease. The bell stand maker suggests that most of the work is done during the meditation process and that after he selects his wood, it requires just some touching up to be made into a flawless bell stand. And the swimmer in roiling water says that he grew up in the water and so is comfortable in it.

Ease is not something that can be directly cultivated. Instead, it is derivative. When one has achieved concentration, letting go, and responsiveness, ease is the visible and felt quality of that achievement. It is in this sense that ease is the most important of the four from the perspective of judging artistic achievement.[50] If ease could not be faked and if high achievement could be produced only from ease, then whenever we witnessed high achievement or the appearance of ease in a somatic art, we would be guaranteed of full aesthetic spontaneity in the artistic process. Unfortunately, ease can be faked and artistic achievement can occur under strain. These facts do not, however, entirely devalue the aesthetic importance of ease. It is still something to be admired and aimed for—indirectly.

For my friend the pianist, who wanted a formula for how to cultivate flow, we can now see that the conceptual tools of aesthetic spontaneity can help in this pursuit. The riddle has not yet been solved, but it has now been made tractable to further study and exploration. Csikszentmihalyi views attention as a kind of psychological capital, something one can invest in through practice and then spend when needed.[51] This suggests a cross-domain view of attention, outside of specific flow experiences. But perhaps the ability to achieve flow in one domain increases the likelihood of achieving it in another. If this is the case, then perhaps we can expand our perspective even further and see aesthetic spontaneity as a kind of *aesthetic capital,* which can be accumulated over time and then unfurled in creative activities.

Epilogue

My contemporary philosophical heroes are Arthur Danto and Nelson Goodman, who were central figures in the field of aesthetics, making significant advances in the field, but who also made important contributions to such fields as philosophy of action, philosophy of language, and philosophical psychology. There is little doubt that their interdisciplinary work was a kind of cross-pollination, where insights from one field led to insights in another. I see comparative philosophy in a similar interdisciplinary light.

Although this book is not a manual on comparative methodology, it is an example (or several examples combined) of comparative methodology. The method is to understand a key philosophical term in its own linguistic and intellectual context and then compare it to related terms or ideas in a different culture in order to (1) recognize the differences, (2) recognize the cascading philosophical implications stemming from the differences, and (3) capitalize on the differences and their implications to make theoretical advances today. A scholar can use this methodology, I believe, to make advances in philosophy using any non-Western or pre-modern linguistic and cultural tradition as a starting point.

Comparative philosophers investigate the fundamental assumptions of texts, philosophers, schools of thought, and entire traditions. These fundamental assumptions, once excavated, help us better understand both the questions that were being asked and the parameters of possible answers. Different assumptions imply different questions and different parameters of possible answers. When similarities arise in different texts, philosophers, schools of thought, or traditions, the mapping of assumptions, questions, and answers will be incomplete, and the gaps will often be more informative than the overlap. But gaps between maps also expose gaps and oversights within maps, and this is where exploring a foreign philosophy can help us better understand our own tradition.

In this book, I first explored the concept of *ziran* in early Chinese philosophy. The exploration detailed in chapter 1 is a simplified restatement of a more technical article called the *Rehabilitation of Spontaneity*.[1] That paper aimed at thoroughly defining *ziran* in a Chinese context but using contemporary terminology in order to set the Chinese ideas up for use in contemporary philosophy of action. That application occurs in a variety of ways in subsequent chapters of this book, which are by and large adaptations of previously published material. In chapter 2, I apply Chinese *ziran* to contemporary philosophy of action though the allied notion of self-organization from the natural sciences. The pathway from the Chinese tradition to contemporary theory has been made more evident in chapter 2 than in the book chapter from which it derives: "Action without Agency and Natural Action: Solving a Double Paradox."

In chapter 3, I again indirectly take the notion of Chinese *ziran* and apply it this time through the notion of effortless attention to contemporary cognitive science. Chapter 3 is a less technical restatement of my introduction to the book *Effortless Attention*[2] plus a summary of a few of the chapters of that volume. In chapter 4, I more directly apply the notion of *ziran* to the field of contemporary aesthetics. Ideas in that chapter have been percolating since my PhD dissertation and have been publicly presented, but only bits and pieces have been previously published. For example, a version of the action diagram was published in the book chapter "Apertures, Draw, and Syntax: Remodeling Attention."[3]

The exploration in this book of the conception of *ziran* helps us see gaps and opportunities in our own tradition, specifically in the fields of philosophy action, philosophical psychology (cognitive science), and aesthetics. But the work I've done here is only a starting point. There are still many more questions to ask and many more answers to be formulated.

I believe that the basic method used in this book can be applied broadly, as a way of using cultural diversity (perspectives and heuristics) to enrich current theory. We can take terms that are endemic to a different tradition, delicately remove them from that tradition, and apply them to our intellectual conversation today. One way to think about this is as a kind of currency exchange. We take New Taiwan dollars, for instance, and change them to American dollars, where they can work for us. Of course, the analogy breaks down in the sense that we still want to preserve some of the characteristics that might make a foreign concept unique as we apply it to a new context. The driving motivation throughout the book is to think of diverse cultures as treasuries of conceptual resources, and this book is just one small example of how that might be possible.

Notes

Introduction

1. This is not meant to diminish the importance of achieving social, political, and economic equity through recognizing the importance of identity diversity. The problems and their solutions are distinct.

2. When the topic of borrowing from other cultures arises, one must be cognizant of the possibility of cultural appropriation, a term that lately implies illegitimate use. Is it illegitimate to use the Chinese notion of *ziran* in a contemporary context? One way to do cross-cultural scholarship is to appreciate components of a foreign culture in their unique context and even to appreciate them for their uniqueness, for their incommensurability, for their having no match in our culture or our time. I am in favor of doing this kind of cross-cultural scholarship. However, it is not the only legitimate way to do cross-cultural scholarship. I am a pluralist when it comes to methods of scholarship and in favor of many approaches thriving at once. This book is an elaboration of one approach—call it *human cross-cultural scholarship*, or *human comparative philosophy*, for its emphasis on taking the distinguishing features of different cultures, recognizing them as part of a common human endeavor—understanding ourselves—and attempting to apply them to the current manifestations of this endeavor, and thereby contributing to and altering the direction of current theory to make it more comprehensive and inclusive. My application of *ziran* to current theory enriches current theory, acknowledges the relevance of early Chinese writings, and opens new avenues of thought and research, without harming the inherent value of the notion in its original context. I love nothing more than exploring the beauty, cleverness, humor, irony, and other qualities of Zhuangzi's writing in the classroom with students of all levels. I also enjoy researching the implications of his ideas for current theory. The two, I submit, are not mutually exclusive and are equally legitimate.

Chapter 1

1. *Shangdi* was a reference to the highest deity in traditional Confucian texts, where it had quite a different sense from Yahweh of the Old and New testaments. The term *tianzhu* was not historically unknown in China but of much lower salience to Confucians, the primary target for Jesuit missionaries. *Tian* means *sky* or *heaven* in Chinese, and *zhu* means *ruler* or *lord*.

2. "*Ziran*" is pronounced *dz-ron*, and "*wuwei*" is pronounced *oo-way*. For the *dz* sound, drop the *ee* sound at the end, so that it sounds sort of like a bee in flight.

3. "Laozi" is pronounced *lou* (like loud)-*dz* (see *ziran* pronunciation above). "Zhuangzi" is pronounced *jwong-dz*. The *j* sound is a straightforward j, as in "jazz" or "jade," not a Frenchified j as in Jacques. (Technically, the *j* sound is of the Chinese *zh* is distinct from the *j* sound of English, but the instructions here provide the closest equivalent.)

4. All translations from the Chinese are mine unless otherwise noted.

5. Wing-tsit Chan, *The Way of Lao Tzu (Tao-Tê Ching)* (Indianapolis: Bobbs-Merrill, 1963).

6. D. C. Lau, *Lao Tzu: Tao Te Ching* (New York: Penguin, 1963).

7. For "action," we could also substitute "motion" or "movement" or "behavior." For "intentionality," we could also substitute "artificiality" or "effort," both of which will be discussed in more detail later in the book.

8. When A. C. Graham first brought these stories to prominence in his translation of the *Zhuangzi* (A. C. Graham, *Chuang-tzŭ: The Inner Chapters* [London: Unwin, 1989]), he referred to them as knack stories. A knack—an innate ability—seems importantly different from a skill—a cultivated ability. Zhuangzi does not say which he means, but he does (as in the first example below) sometimes imply a process of cultivation. And to the extent that any skill requires honing and practice, it seems fair to characterize the stories as skill stories rather than as knack stories. We see this process of cultivation in the most famous skill story in the *Zhuangzi* (ch. 3), the story of the butcher who carves up a beef carcass with such ease and dexterity that it attracts the attention of a nobleman. The butcher relates a process spanning more than a decade in which he gradually improves his butchering skill.

9. *Tian* 天 is one of the most interesting and complex terms in early Chinese philosophy, with no direct equivalent in the West. It seems to combine two ideas that are entirely incompatible in dominant traditions of Western metaphysics: heaven and nature. The earliest meaning of *tian* was *sky*, which it can still mean today. In that it can also have a deistic sense of spiritual intervention in human lives, it has a slight analogue in the Western conception of heaven. In the West, this idea branched off into an entirely different realm that acquired a sense of ontological priority over its opposite—the natural

realm. In China, that split never occurred, and so the natural and the heavenly theoretically remain unified.

10. The notion of concentration will be important in chapters 2 and 3, where it is discussed as a high level of attention, but it is fair to ask at this point why *ziran* necessarily involves attention. After all, as a description of natural processes, it seems clear that nature does not concentrate attention in the same way that a human mind does. Chapter 2 goes some way in responding to this objection by peeling self-consciousness off from the process. *Ziran* in nature clearly does not involve self-consciousness, and neither does it in humans. Concentration without self-consciousness is a bit mysterious. What does it mean to concentrate if I am not aware that I am doing it? Simply put, concentration, or attention, is a coordination of cognitive resources on a particular set of external or internal stimuli. But if nature doesn't have cognitive resources per se, how does *ziran* as concentration apply to it? The question is actually easier to answer than it might appear and the reason it appears difficult is that we have a reflex to separate humans from nature (again, see chapter 2). If we include humans as among all things natural, we can quickly conclude that the manifestation of *ziran* in humans includes concentration, but its manifestation elsewhere in nature may not. *Ziran* is a description of process, which may manifest distinctly in distinct systems. I do not claim that *ziran* necessarily involves concentration in nonhuman nature.

11. Some scholars take Zhuangzi to be an out and out skeptic, meaning that he has no position of his own about how we acquire knowledge or about ethical norms or about how one should lead one's life, etc. I think this is an error and that Zhuangzi does believe that *ziran/wu-wei* is an ideal form of action. After all, he extols this kind of action without problematizing it, whereas he repeatedly problematizes types of action that adhere to social convention. Zhuangzi, in my view, is a skeptic about convention (including language and the knowledge derived from it) but not a skeptic in the Pyrrhonian style.

12. At Eastern Michigan University, where the Philosophy and History programs are combined under the umbrella of one department, and some students take multiple classes in both fields, there is sometimes some confusion among students about what distinguishes the work of intellectual historians and philosophers working in the history of ideas. The distinction mentioned here is just one of several and is not in any way meant as a value judgment.

13. Hippocrates G. Apostle and Lloyd P. Gerson, *Aristotle: Selected Works* (St. Merrimack, NH: Peripatetic Press, 1991). I've replaced two terms with Roman alphabet transcription of the original Greek.

14. Apostle and Gerson, *Aristotle: Selected Works*.

15. Aristotle, *Physics, Book VIII*, trans. Daniel W. Graham (Oxford: Clarendon, 1999).

16. It is unnecessary and unwarranted to view the contrasts among Aristotle and the Daoists as if they represent mutually exclusive positions. Neither Aristotle nor the Daoists would be so simpleminded as to say there is always only one best way of doing anything. The contrasts I am pointing out here are tendencies to value certain ways of thinking and acting. Aristotle favors deliberative thinking (likely because of his emphasis on ethics), and Daoists favor responsive action. This does not mean that Daoists would necessarily dismiss the value of deliberation or that Aristotle would necessarily denigrate responsive action. It is important not to overstate the differences in emphasis, but it is equally important not to gloss them over. The different conceptions of action deeply influenced later generations.

17. The problem I'm presenting here in terms of action and nature in Aristotle cannot be found in any current history of philosophy. In fact, scholars of Aristotle will likely be dumbfounded to learn that Aristotle separates humans from nature, because he conceived of the human being as a rational animal, in contrast to his teacher Plato. My argument, however, focuses on action and its origins. This is where Aristotle does, in fact, separate humans from nature. He must do this in order to get to responsibility. He does not posit a clear determinism/freedom dichotomy, but both ideas (or ideas very like them) are latent in his philosophy, such that in order to have moral responsibility, humans must be able to free ourselves from the bounds of natural causality. One of the benefits of using non-Western concepts as a mirror for our own is that they allow new perspectives on old ideas.

18. None of the many full-length treatises (written in Greek) by Epicurus or Chrysippus survive. I am following their later Latin expositions.

19. The term *physical* is difficult to apply directly to Chinese philosophy. What I mean by it is that there was no physical/spiritual dichotomy. In early China, although talk of *qi* 氣 (a kind of energy that also possessed materiality) and *shen* 神 (often translated as *spirit* or *god*) was common, it was understood that these were metaphysically continuous with the material world and not of a separate realm. Metaphysical ideas in early China were not entirely explicit, but there seemed to more or less be a consensus that everything is composed of *qi* at different densities. Rocks were dense with *qi*, whereas spirits were diaphanous.

20. Jean Jacques Rousseau, *Emile, or On Education*, trans. Allan Bloom (New York: Basic Books, 1979), 285.

21. You can see this most easily by thinking about the term *tian* 天, which means both *natural* and *heavenly*, as discussed above.

22. William James, *The Principles of Psychology* (Cambridge: Harvard University Press, 1983), 1174.

23. James, *Principles of Psychology*, 1169.

24. Friedrich Schiller, Jane Veronica Curran, and Christophe Fricker, *Schiller's "On Grace and Dignity" (1793) in Its Cultural Context: Essays and a New Translation* (Columbia, SC: Camden House, 2005), 145–146.

25. Schiller, Curran, and Fricker, 146.
26. Schiller, Curran, and Fricker, 166.
27. I am taking Laozi and Zhuangzi to have naturalistic assumptions. One might reasonably object that because they broach the notion of spirit (*shen* 神) and souls, it is an issue worth further exploration. My view is that a close examination of the texts will show that the notion of *shen* is not outside of a naturalist purview and refers to the unexpected (outside of immediate human understanding) rather than to the truly anomalous. Similarly, their notion of souls most likely has a metaphysical basis in *qi* 氣, rather than a divine basis outside of nature altogether. See also note 16 above.

Chapter 2

1. Malcolm Budd, "The Aesthetic Appreciation of Nature," *The British Journal of Aesthetics* 36, no. 3 (July 1, 1996): 207–22, https://doi.org/10.1093/bjaesthetics/36.3.207, p. 208.

2. Emily Brady, "Imagination and the Aesthetic Appreciation of Nature," *The Journal of Aesthetics and Art Criticism* 56, no. 2 (1998): 139–47, https://doi.org/10.2307/432252, p. 139.

3. Holmes Rolston, "Aesthetic Experience in Forests," *The Journal of Aesthetics and Art Criticism* 56, no. 2 (1998): 157–66, https://doi.org/10.2307/432254, p. 160.

4. Of course, the idea of determinism is very useful in fields such as physical mechanics and engineering, allowing us to do such things as send spaceships out into the solar system and even intercept a comet. I'm not denying this aspect of determinism in common physics. Whether determinism can be extended to every organizational level and every aspect of nature, however, is currently an unsettled question.

5. There are countless books and articles dedicated to what philosophers of action call *compatibility* between determinism and freedom in humans, but after two thousand years, we are still very far from a consensus opinion.

6. Gerald Borgia, "Bower Quality, Number of Decorations and Mating Success of Male Satin Bowerbirds (Ptilonorhynchus Violaceus): An Experimental Analysis," *Animal Behaviour* 33, no. 1 (Feb. 1, 1985): 266–71, https://doi.org/10.1016/S0003-3472(85)80140-8, p. 266.

7. Robert Aunger, "What's Special about Human Technology?" *Cambridge Journal of Economics* 34, no. 1 (Jan. 1, 2010): 115–123, https://doi.org/10.1093/cje/bep018, p. 117.

8. Again, a dogmatic philosopher might be skeptical of this move because it again looks like a category mistake—instead of talking about a metaphysical concept, we are talking about the language that describes our metaphysics. This is a category mistake only if one is unaware that one is doing it and one is

making unfounded claims about metaphysics by confusing the terms and the objects referred to by the terms. I am here looking at language specifically as a way to understand our metaphysics better. I'm not saying that our language determines our metaphysics, simply that our language can plausibly give us hints about our metaphysics.

9. Of course, there are more parts to a plant than just the sexual parts, and the sexual parts and processes are more complex than depicted here, so properly speaking, there should be more letters and more verbs, but here we are trying to understand a complex process through a schematized example of self-organized motion. To see more complex processes of self-organized motion in plants, look up videos for leaf stomata or CO_2 transport in plants.

10. Are there, metaphysically speaking, really two kinds of selves? That we generally assume there to be is sufficient for my argument, which is about our assumed metaphysics (as revealed through the language we use), not about absolute metaphysical truth.

11. Some philosophers say that the mental act itself counts as an action, but we are concerned here with actual external motion, not just with what is going on in the mind.

12. Amir Raz and Natasha K. J. Campbell, "Can Suggestion Obviate Reading? Supplementing Primary Stroop Evidence with Exploratory Negative Priming Analyses," *Consciousness and Cognition* 20, no. 2 (2011): 312–20, https://doi.org/10.1016/j.concog.2009.09.013.

13. Raz and Campbell report (ibid.) that the Stroop facilitation effect vanishes under suggestion for highly suggestive individuals (HSIs) (which is true by the technical definition, comparing it to the neutral trials), but there was still some facilitation. According to Raz and Campbell's results, the difference in reaction time (RT) between the congruent and incongruent trials for HSIs is statistically significant. Furthermore, in this and another study (Amir Raz, Jin Fan, and Michael I. Posner, "Hypnotic Suggestion Reduces Conflict in the Human Brain," *Proceedings of the National Academy of Sciences* 102, no. 28 (July 12, 2005): 9978–83, https://doi.org/10.1073/pnas.0503064102), the RT for HSIs in congruent trials dropped under suggestion, dramatically so in "Hypnotic Suggestion." These two sets of results indicate that there is still a significant amount of reading going on.

14. I wonder if eventually the idea will vanish entirely from Chinese textbooks under American and European influence. If so, it would be unfortunate.

15. Mihaly Csikszentmihalyi, *Beyond Boredom and Anxiety* (San Francisco: Jossey-Bass, 1975), 86–87.

Chapter 3

1. Properly speaking, the "cognitive sciences" include philosophy of mind, so we have not really left the field of philosophy.

2. Because Kahneman wrote the book about it (Daniel Kahneman, *Attention and Effort* [Englewood Cliffs: Prentice-Hall, 1973]), I'll use his name as shorthand for quite a number of psychology researchers in his day who used similar methods to study attention and effort.

3. In physics, there is a distinction between effort force (the force, for example, exerted on the near end of a lever) and the load force (the force exerted against the load itself by the far end of the lever). Thus, in regard to objective effort in the realm of physics, it is possible to have low effort force and high load force. Might there also be such a distinction in regard to cognitive effort?

4. Lionel Naccache et al., "Effortless Control: Executive Attention and Conscious Feeling of Mental Effort Are Dissociable," *Neuropsychologia* 43, no. 9 (2005): 1318–28, https://doi.org/10.1016/j.neuropsychologia.2004.11.024.

5. C. Prablanc and D. Pélisson, "Gaze Saccade Orienting and Hand Pointing Are Locked to Their Goal by Quick Internal Loops," in *Attention and Performance XIII: Motor Representation and Control*, ed. Marc Jeannerod (Hillsdale, NJ: Lawrence Erlbaum, 1990), 653–76.

6. Bernhard Hommel, "Grounding Attention in Action Control," in *Effortless Attention: A New Perspective in the Cognitive Science of Action and Attention*, ed. Brian Bruya (Cambridge: MIT Press, 2010), 121–40, 136.

7. Although this research suggests that symptoms of ADHD can be improved by both parents and child, it does not necessarily imply that symptoms of ADHD in a child are the fault of the parent or the child.

Chapter 4

1. Yee Chiang, *Chinese Calligraphy: An Introduction to Its Aesthetic and Technique* (Cambridge: Harvard University Press, 1976), 110.

2. R. Keith Sawyer, "Improvisation and the Creative Process: Dewey, Collingwood, and the Aesthetics of Spontaneity," *The Journal of Aesthetics and Art Criticism* 58, no. 2 (2000): 149–61, https://doi.org/10.2307/432094.

3. James O. Young and Carl Matheson, "The Metaphysics of Jazz," *The Journal of Aesthetics and Art Criticism* 58, no. 2 (2000): 125–33, https://doi.org/10.2307/432091.

4. Richard Cochrane, "Playing by the Rules: A Pragmatic Characterization of Musical Performances," *The Journal of Aesthetics and Art Criticism* 58, no. 2 (2000): 135–42, https://doi.org/10.2307/432092.

5. Carol S. Gould and Kenneth Keaton, "The Essential Role of Improvisation in Musical Performance," *The Journal of Aesthetics and Art Criticism* 58, no. 2 (2000): 143–48, https://doi.org/10.2307/432093.

6. Philip Alperson, "On Musical Improvisation," *The Journal of Aesthetics and Art Criticism* 43, no. 1 (1984): 17–29, https://doi.org/10.2307/430189.

7. For this chapter, I surveyed a broad range of articles and books on improvisation and focus here on a set mostly taken from special issue of

the *Journal of Aesthetics and Art Criticism*. The articles are wide ranging and represent a nice cross-section of all the available literature on improvisation before and since.

8. It is worth emphasizing that by saying that the West has something to learn from the Chinese tradition, I am not saying that the Western tradition is inherently deficient or that the Chinese tradition is inherently superior. Rather, in the spirit of humility and the desire to take advantage of cultural diversity as cognitive diversity, it is an attempt to move our ideas forward. For the last century in China, the Chinese have been borrowing ideas from the West, often with more than a tinge of resentment, but we should set feelings of resentment aside as well as thoughts of superiority and inferiority. We are all humans trying to make progress on human problems, even if they and some of the resources to solve them are culturally situated.

9. At this point the reader might object at attempting to use the Confucian six arts as a resource for explaining a Daoist theory of aesthetics. Why should one school of thought be used to explain a theory from a rival school of thought? The clear separation of Confucianism and Daoism has always been tentative and fraught. Although differences can surely be found in coarse descriptions of their ethics and politics—Daoists, for example, had little patience for niceties of ritual propriety—there is also much that unites them, and one field that represents this unity more than any other is the field of aesthetics.

10. Bernard Karlgren, "Grammata Serica Recensa," *Bulletin of Far Eastern Antiquities* 29 (1957): 1–332, 98.

11. Chiang, *Chinese Calligraphy*, 111. I am using Chiang Yee as a stand-in for the many other works in the long tradition of aesthetics and art criticism in China. My understanding is that what he is saying is generally true of the tradition, and so instead of painstakingly cataloging quotations from classic texts to document this, which would be well beyond the scope of this chapter, I am using Chiang Yee as a kind of shorthand.

12. Art (*ars*) in ancient Rome, and commonly across the European tradition, was often understood as fundamentally mimetic, that is, as a form of imitation—imitation of nature. In the Chinese tradition, by contrast, it is an *enactment* of nature. As natural movement, art in the Chinese tradition *is* nature, not just an artificial reproduction of nature.

13. Chiang, *Chinese Calligraphy*, 112.

14. Chiang, *Chinese Calligraphy*, 112.

15. Chiang, *Chinese Calligraphy*, 113.

16. Mihaly Csikszentmihalyi, *Flow: The Psychology of Optimal Experience* (New York: Harper Perennial, 2008).

17. The notion of somatic art described here is related to but distinct from Richard Shusterman's idea of somaesthetics. One could say that the somatic arts are a branch of the much broader category of somaesthetics.

18. In the allographic arts, there is an important distinction between composition and instantiation (which is often a performance). For example, the art of dance involves creative artistry on the part of the choreographer in the creation of the dance and on the part of the dancers in their dancing. Other relevant allographic arts are music and drama. See Nelson Goodman, *Languages of Art: An Approach to a Theory of Symbols* (Indianapolis: Hackett, 1976).

19. Lothar Ledderose, *Mi Fu and the Classical Tradition of Chinese Calligraphy* (Princeton: Princeton University Press, 1979), 29.

20. I note in chapter 1 some interesting parallels between Schiller's notion of spontaneity in grace and the Daoist notion of *ziran*. I also note that Schiller derives the framing of his ideas from Kant. There are also fascinating parallels between Kant's aesthetic theory and the ideas that are developed in this chapter. In both chapters 1 and 2, I intentionally ignore similarities between Kant's vocabulary and the vocabulary in this book because the conceptual similarities are more apparent than real. In his third critique, Kant discusses how art achieves a kind of purposiveness without purpose. In translations of Kant's work, we see terms such as *spontaneity, nature,* and *purposiveness without purpose* and begin to suspect that the ideas may be quite similar to Zhuangzi's. In fact, they are quite different. Spontaneity, for Kant, is caught up in the paradox of spontaneity, on the side of free will (though complicated by his complex idea of transcendentalism). Nature, for Kant, is caught up on the other side—in determinism (transcendentally so), but with an appearance of design—which is what he means by "purposiveness." So "purposiveness without purpose" for Kant is not anything like nonaction; rather, it is a clarification of what he means by purposiveness, which is to say that something—namely, nature—has the appearance of having been designed, it appears to always be working toward ends, as opposed to functioning randomly or with an actual design from an actual intentional creator. Artistic genius, for Kant, is the ability to create purposiveness in art but make it seem free of the overt intention to do so—the semblance of nature's purposiveness without purpose. I am indebted to Christian Wenzel for personal conversations on this topic. See his *An Introduction to Kant's Aesthetics: Core Concepts and Problems* (Malden: Blackwell, 2005). See also Immanuel Kant and J. H Bernard, *Kant's Critique of Judgement* (London: Macmillan, 1914).

21. Alastair Macaulay, "Review: A Mark Morris Premiere Features Singular Theater Poetry," *New York Times*, May 18, 2016, https://www.nytimes.com/2016/05/19/arts/dance/review-a-mark-morris-premiere-features-singular-theater-poetry.html.

22. Gia Kourlas, "Extending the Reach of a Long Run, Twists Included," *New York Times*, March 23, 2014. https://www.nytimes.com/2014/03/24/arts/dance/paul-taylor-dance-at-koch-theater.html

23. Chiang, *Chinese Calligraphy*, 111.

24. *Gu hua pin lu* 古畫品錄. I don't deny that there have been a variety of opinions regarding aesthetic worth throughout the long Chinese tradition, nor do I deny that there have been multiple interpretations of terms such as *shen* and *qi*. Nevertheless, there has also been a remarkable staying power of these terms as descriptors of aesthetic worth. It should also be noted that the term *emotional energy* is not foreign to contemporary Western painting, but it is interesting to see how it is used differently. In somatic arts, it is used to describe the performances of dancers and musicians. In painting, it often refers to something invested in the art by the artist—with the notable exception of Jackson Pollock and other so-called action painters. Compare, for example, the following two descriptions of the painter partners Lee Krasner (not an action painter) and Pollock. "Lee Krasner . . . was free to invest in her painting the emotional energy that as his helpmate she had never allowed full rein" (Grace Glueck, "Art: Lee Krasner Finds Her Place in Retrospective at Modern," *New York Times*, December 21, 1984, https://www.nytimes.com/1984/12/21/arts/art-lee-krasner-finds-her-place-in-retrospective-ar-modern.html). "The paint holds the emotional energy of [Pollock's] action" (Cynthia Shaltzman, "At the Met New York Painting and Sculpture 1940–1970 at the New York Metropolitan Museum of Art until February 1," *The Harvard Crimson*, December 11, 1969, https://www.thecrimson.com/article/1969/12/11/at-the-met-new-york-painting/).

25. By this point, the reader should associate "professional calligrapher" from China with high art and not with graphic design.

26. "*Qi*" is pronounced *chee*.

27. The relationship between a subjective feeling of ease and an objective appearance of ease deserves further exploration. When I have raised this issue in talks, audience members have said that ballet dancers, for example, may be struggling internally at the very limits of their endurance while projecting a pretense of ease. It makes sense to me, however, that a ballet dancer who is actually at ease while performing at a high level will look more graceful—more natural—than one who is struggling internally and merely projecting a sense of ease. That genuine sense of ease, I contend, will be aesthetically appreciated more than the affected sense of ease, all else being equal.

28. See the documentary film, Kim Evans, *Jackson Pollock* (Framingham, MA: RM Arts, 1987).

29. See note 7 above.

30. Sawyer sets improvisational creativity off against product creativity (e.g., an original painting), claiming that the latter is the paradigmatic case of aesthetic appreciation and the former, though being quite pervasive (as the basis of everyday conversation, for example), is comparatively neglected by scholars. It's also worth stating that although the example of Picasso is of an individual working in his studio, Sawyer's understanding of improvisational creativity is generally that it is collaborative and public. The use of Picasso by

Sawyer emphasizes the compositional aspect, which is most relevant to the discussion here.

31. William Day, "Knowing as Instancing: Jazz Improvisation and Moral Perfectionism," *The Journal of Aesthetics and Art Criticism* 58, no. 2 (2000): 99–111, https://doi.org/10.2307/432089.

32. Day's emphasis is on moral perfection (with specific reference to Emerson and Kant), but everyday improvisation plays a key role in his article. The topic also arises in several other articles. See also Garry Hagberg, *Art as Language: Wittgenstein, Meaning, and Aesthetic Theory* (Ithaca: Cornell University Press, 1995).

33. Lee B. Brown, "'Feeling My Way': Jazz Improvisation and Its Vicissitudes—A Plea for Imperfection," *The Journal of Aesthetics and Art Criticism* 58, no. 2 (2000): 113–23, https://doi.org/10.2307/432090.

34. Brown, "'Feeling My Way,'" 121.

35. John C. Gilmour, "Improvisation in Cézanne's Late Landscapes," *The Journal of Aesthetics and Art Criticism* 58, no. 2 (2000): 191–204, https://doi.org/10.2307/432098.

36. Curtis L. Carter, "Improvisation in Dance," *The Journal of Aesthetics and Art Criticism* 58, no. 2 (2000): 181–90, https://doi.org/10.2307/432097.

37. David Sterritt, "Revision, Prevision, and the Aura of Improvisatory Art," *The Journal of Aesthetics and Art Criticism* 58, no. 2 (2000): 163–72, https://doi.org/10.2307/432095.

38. It is important to note that the category of compositional improvisation is mine and might be disavowed by the authors to whom I am attributing it. Although their main emphasis may not be on the compositional aspect of improvisation, I am claiming that this is implicitly part of their theory. Sawyer, for example, discusses the importance of what he calls ready-mades (e.g., clichés) and constraints, but his view of the creativity of improvisation, on my reading, is that it involves creativity that is equivalent to a composer or writer sitting at a table writing a script or score. The differences between an improviser and a sit-down author, following Sawyer, is that improvisation occurs live, in the moment, is not open to revision, and is often collaborative. Fundamentally, however, both create compositions. This is distinct from interpretation or elaboration, in which the composition itself already exists and the creativity of the improvisation is derived from that preexisting composition.

39. One should be careful not to confuse the compositional/derivative distinction with a distinction Brown refers to between retrospective and prospective. The key to understanding the compositional/derivative distinction is to think in terms of an opus and to understand that both compositional and derivative are forms of improvisation. In compositional improvisation, the artist is creating an opus on the fly, impromptu. In derivative improvisation, the opus already exists, and the improviser is working from that (additionally,

derivative improvisation can mean to improvise from convention). The key to the retrospective/prospective distinction is not about the opus per se but about the temporal direction of one's attention and understanding that only the retrospective model counts as improvisation. In the retrospective model, the improviser looks backward in time, say at a collaborator's prior lick, and then creates from that. From a compositional/derivative perspective, working retrospectively could be either compositional or derivative, depending on whether a score already exists. In the prospective model, a score already exists, and the musician is looking forward in time to the coming notes on the score. In the compositional/derivative distinction, following Gould and Keaton, the musician's looking forward will also necessarily be a kind of improvisation, as not all musical features can be captured in a score. In Brown's retrospective/prospective distinction, the prospective does not count as improvisation.

40. One shouldn't take the word *nothing* too far here. Of course, there will still be recognizable conventions, methods, styles, building blocks, etc.

41. Barry Kernfeld provides a discussion of kinds of jazz improvisation from a musicological perspective, identifying three categories of improvisatory technique: paraphrase ("strict, bar-by-bar embellishment of pre-existing material in such a way that it remains recognizable"), formulaic ("proceeds by means of the ingenious weaving together of fragments from a general repertory that is common to many diverse pieces"), and motivic ("one or more themes from the basis for a section of a piece, an entire piece, or a group of related pieces . . . developed through . . . such processes as ornamentation, transposition, rhythmic displacement, diminution, augmentation, and inversion"), plus modal improvisation (which "explores the melodic and harmonic possibilities of a collection of pitches . . . expressed harmonically through drones or through two or more chords that oscillate beneath melodic lines using the same pitches"). See Barry Kernfeld, "Improvisation (Jazz)," in *Grove Music Online*, https://doi.org/10.1093/gmo/9781561592630.article.J215000.

42. A different interpretation of the articles in question might result in discord rather than harmony among the various perspectives on improvisation. I referred above to Brown's use of the notions of situation, forced choice, and unscripted. If one were to consider these a package and claim that this package is a necessary condition of improvisation, it would then preclude certain views of improvisation, such as Carter and Gilmour's view of improvisation away from convention and Gould and Keaton's view of improvisation in classical music (which is scripted), and even Sawyer's Picasso, who is not situated and has the luxury of revision. Classifying Brown's view as compositional is essentially an aesthetic choice of my own, preferring harmony over discord.

43. Sterritt, for example, quotes Kerouac's description of the writing process: "excitedly, swiftly, with writing-or-typing-cramps, in accordance . . . with the laws of orgasm" (Sterritt, "Revision, Prevision," 167).

44. "100 percent personal honesty both psychic and social etc." (Sterritt, "Revision, Prevision," 167).

45. In the same vein, Kandinsky used the word *improvisation* for "spontaneous expressions of incidents of an inner character, or impression of the 'inner nature'" (Wassily Kandinsky, *Concerning the Spiritual in Art* [New York: Guggenheim Foundation, 1946], 98).

46. Evans, *Jackson Pollock*.

47. Stemming from Kant's distinction between regulative and constitutive principles and following Elisabeth Anscombe and John Rawls, John Searle was the first to articulate the distinction between constitutive rules and regulatory rules. Searle does so in the broad context of institutions, particularly as they pertain to linguistic practices but defines them specifically in terms of activities: "Regulative rules regulate activities whose existence is independent of the rules; constitutive rules constitute (and also regulate) forms of activity 'whose existence is logically dependent on the rules'" (John R. Searle, "How to Derive 'Ought' From 'Is,'" *The Philosophical Review* 73, no. 1 (1964): 43–58, https://doi.org/10.2307/2183201, p. 55).

48. The term I am interpreting as to lose awareness is *jue* 厥. A common reading of this term is as a substitute for a phonologically and orthographically similar term, namely, *jue* 橛, which means severed or split and which appears in an almost identical passage in the text *Liezi*. Whatever the exact interpretation of the term, the metaphor appears to be one of an absence of self-consciousness and in this sense can be equated with several similar passages in the *Zhuangzi* that refer to a calm mind as being like dead or wet ash. In fact, in chapter 24, the very same passage that appears after the passage in question in the *Zhuangzi* precedes a passage that refers to the mind as dead ash. Compare 吾處身也若厥株拘，吾執臂也若槁木之枝 in chapter 19 to 身若槁木之枝而心若死灰 in chapter 24.

49. Match nature with nature: *yi tian he tian* 以天合天.

50. In discussing the unscripted feature of postmodern dance, Curtis Carter says, "These circumstances raise what may be the crucial question for improvisation, that is, the question of how to evaluate the product. Improvisational dance would require different criteria of assessment from preset works, which minimally rely on such measures as compliance with a preexisting set of features, formal richness of structure, or possibly the range and intensity of expressiveness. Perhaps such values as change, flow, and risk may be more useful in evaluating improvisational dance than traditional criteria." Carter, "Improvisation in Dance," 189.

51. "'Capital is developed through a pattern of investment of psychic resources that results in obtaining experiential rewards from the present moment while also increasing the likelihood of future benefit,' [Csikszentmihalyi] said. 'And, in psychology, the primary resource is not money, is not power—it's

attention to topics of present and future value.'" Karen Kersting, "Turning Happiness into Economic Power," *Monitor on Psychology*, December 2003, www.apa.org/monitor/dec03/power.

Epilogue

1. Brian J. Bruya, "The Rehabilitation of Spontaneity: A New Approach in Philosophy of Action," *Philosophy East and West* 60, no. 2 (2010): 207–50.

2. Brian Bruya, ed., *Effortless Attention: A New Perspective in the Cognitive Science of Attention and Action* (Cambridge: MIT Press, 2010).

3. Brian Bruya, "Apertures, Draw, and Syntax: Remodeling Attention," in *Effortless Attention*, 219–45.

Works Cited

Alperson, Philip. "On Musical Improvisation." *The Journal of Aesthetics and Art Criticism* 43, no. 1 (1984): 17–29. https://doi.org/10.2307/430189.
Aristotle. *Physics, Book VIII.* Translated by Daniel W. Graham. Oxford: Clarendon, 1999.
Aunger, Robert. "What's Special about Human Technology?" *Cambridge Journal of Economics* 34, no. 1 (January 1, 2010): 115–23. https://doi.org/10.1093/cje/bep018.
Borgia, Gerald. "Bower Quality, Number of Decorations and Mating Success of Male Satin Bowerbirds (Ptilonorhynchus Violaceus): An Experimental Analysis." *Animal Behaviour* 33, no. 1 (February 1, 1985): 266–71. https://doi.org/10.1016/S0003-3472(85)80140-8.
Brady, Emily. "Imagination and the Aesthetic Appreciation of Nature." *The Journal of Aesthetics and Art Criticism* 56, no. 2 (1998): 139–47. https://doi.org/10.2307/432252.
Brown, Lee B. " 'Feeling My Way': Jazz Improvisation and Its Vicissitudes–A Plea for Imperfection." *The Journal of Aesthetics and Art Criticism* 58, no. 2 (2000): 113–23. https://doi.org/10.2307/432090.
Bruya, Brian. "Apertures, Draw, and Syntax: Remodelling Attention." In *Effortless Attention: A New Perspective in the Cognitive Science of Attention and Action*, 219–245. Cambridge: MIT Press, 2010.
———, ed. *Effortless Attention: A New Perspective in the Cognitive Science of Attention and Action.* Cambridge: MIT Press, 2010.
———. "The Rehabilitation of Spontaneity: A New Approach in Philosophy of Action." *Philosophy East and West* 60, no. 2 (2010): 207–50.
———. "Aesthetic Spontaneity: A Theory of Action Based on Affective Responsiveness." PhD diss. University of Hawai'i, 2004.
Budd, Malcolm. "The Aesthetic Appreciation of Nature." *The British Journal of Aesthetics* 36, no. 3 (July 1, 1996): 207–22. https://doi.org/10.1093/bjaesthetics/36.3.207.

Carter, Curtis L. "Improvisation in Dance." *The Journal of Aesthetics and Art Criticism* 58, no. 2 (2000): 181–90. https://doi.org/10.2307/432097.
Chiang, Yee. *Chinese Calligraphy: An Introduction to Its Aesthetic and Technique.* Cambridge: Harvard University Press, 1976.
Cochrane, Richard. "Playing by the Rules: A Pragmatic Characterization of Musical Performances." *The Journal of Aesthetics and Art Criticism* 58, no. 2 (2000): 135–42. https://doi.org/10.2307/432092.
Csikszentmihalyi, Mihaly. *Beyond Boredom and Anxiety.* San Francisco: Jossey-Bass, 1975.
———. *Flow: The Psychology of Optimal Experience.* New York: Harper Perennial, 2008.
Day, William. "Knowing as Instancing: Jazz Improvisation and Moral Perfectionism." *The Journal of Aesthetics and Art Criticism* 58, no. 2 (2000): 99–111. https://doi.org/10.2307/432089.
Evans, Kim. *Jackson Pollock.* Framingham, MA: RM Arts, 1987.
Gilmour, John C. "Improvisation in Cézanne's Late Landscapes." *The Journal of Aesthetics and Art Criticism* 58, no. 2 (2000): 191–204. https://doi.org/10.2307/432098.
Goodman, Nelson. *Languages of Art: An Approach to a Theory of Symbols.* Indianapolis: Hackett, 1976.
Gould, Carol S., and Kenneth Keaton. "The Essential Role of Improvisation in Musical Performance." *The Journal of Aesthetics and Art Criticism* 58, no. 2 (2000): 143–48. https://doi.org/10.2307/432093.
Graham, A. C. *Chuang-tzŭ: The Inner Chapters.* London: Unwin, 1989.
Hagberg, Garry. *Art as Language: Wittgenstein, Meaning, and Aesthetic Theory.* Ithaca: Cornell University Press, 1995.
Hommel, Bernhard. "Grounding Attention in Action Control." In *Effortless Attention: A New Perspective in the Cognitive Science of Action and Attention,* ed. Brian Bruya, 121–40. Cambridge: MIT Press, 2010.
James, William. *The Principles of Psychology.* Cambridge: Harvard University Press, 1983.
Kahneman, Daniel. *Attention and Effort.* Englewood Cliffs, NJ: Prentice-Hall, 1973.
Kandinsky, Wassily. *Concerning the Spiritual in Art.* New York: Guggenheim Foundation, 1946.
Karlgren, Bernard. "Grammata Serica Recensa." *Bulletin of Far Eastern Antiquities* 29 (1957): 1–332.
Kernfeld, Barry. "Improvisation (Jazz)." In *Grove Music Online.* Accessed June 28, 2020. https://doi.org/10.1093/gmo/9781561592630.article.J215000.
Kersting, Karen. "Turning Happiness into Economic Power." *Monitor on Psychology,* December 2003. www.apa.org/monitor/dec03/power.
Laozi, and Wing-tsit Chan. *The Way of Lao Tzu (Tao-Tê Ching).* Indianapolis: Bobbs-Merrill, 1963.

Lau, D. C. *Lao Tzu: Tao Te Ching*. New York: Penguin Books, 1963.
Ledderose, Lothar. *Mi Fu and the Classical Tradition of Chinese Calligraphy*. Princeton: Princeton University Press, 1979.
Naccache, Lionel, Stanislas Dehaene, Laurent Cohen, Marie-Odile Habert, Elodie Guichart-Gomez, Damien Galanaud, and Jean-Claude Willer. "Effortless Control: Executive Attention and Conscious Feeling of Mental Effort Are Dissociable." *Neuropsychologia* 43, no. 9 (2005): 1318–28. https://doi.org/10.1016/j.neuropsychologia.2004.11.024.
Prablanc, C., and D. Pélisson. "Gaze Saccade Orienting and Hand Pointing Are Locked to Their Goal by Quick Internal Loops." In *Attention and Performance XIII: Motor Representation and Control*, ed. Marc Jeannerod, 653–76. Hillsdale, NJ: Lawrence Erlbaum, 1990.
Raz, Amir, and Natasha K. J. Campbell. "Can Suggestion Obviate Reading? Supplementing Primary Stroop Evidence with Exploratory Negative Priming Analyses." *Consciousness and Cognition: An International Journal* 20, no. 2 (2011): 312–20. https://doi.org/10.1016/j.concog.2009.09.013.
Raz, Amir, Jin Fan, and Michael I. Posner. "Hypnotic Suggestion Reduces Conflict in the Human Brain." *Proceedings of the National Academy of Sciences* 102, no. 28 (July 12, 2005): 9978–83. https://doi.org/10.1073/pnas.0503064102.
Rolston, Holmes. "Aesthetic Experience in Forests." *The Journal of Aesthetics and Art Criticism* 56, no. 2 (1998): 157–66. https://doi.org/10.2307/432254.
Rousseau, Jean Jacques, and Allan David Bloom. *Emile, or On Education*. New York: Basic Books, 1979.
Sawyer, R. Keith. "Improvisation and the Creative Process: Dewey, Collingwood, and the Aesthetics of Spontaneity." *The Journal of Aesthetics and Art Criticism* 58, no. 2 (2000): 149. https://doi.org/10.2307/432094.
Schiller, Friedrich, Jane Veronica Curran, and Christophe Fricker. *Schiller's "On Grace and Dignity" (1793) in Its Cultural Context: Essays and a New Translation*. Columbia, SC: Camden House, 2005.
Searle, John R. "How to Derive 'Ought' From 'Is.'" *The Philosophical Review* 73, no. 1 (1964): 43–58. https://doi.org/10.2307/2183201.
Sterritt, David. "Revision, Prevision, and the Aura of Improvisatory Art." *The Journal of Aesthetics and Art Criticism* 58, no. 2 (2000): 163–72. https://doi.org/10.2307/432095.
Wenzel, Christian Helmut. *An Introduction to Kant's Aesthetics: Core Concepts and Problems*. Malden, MA: Blackwell, 2005.
Young, James O., and Carl Matheson. "The Metaphysics of Jazz." *The Journal of Aesthetics and Art Criticism* 58, no. 2 (2000): 125–33. https://doi.org/10.2307/432091.

Index

Locators in *italic* refer to tables and figures.

action
   action syntax as an aspect of effortless attention, 78–79
   in Daoism. *See* natural action in Daoism
   phenomenal agency and volition required in thinking of action in the West, 54–55, 98, 132n11
   in Western philosophy. *See* philosophy of action
   See also spontaneity
aesthetics
   appreciation of nature aesthetically, 42–43
   and the Confucian six arts (*liu yi* 六藝), 94–95, 97, 134n9
   emotional energy, 100, 136n24
   of natural human action, 43, 46
   questions related to appreciation of art, 41–42
   somaesthetics. *See* somatic art
aesthetic spontaneity
   as a distinguishing mark of artistry in the somatic arts, 102–104, 111
   four aspects of nature-as-movement associated with summarized, 103, 107, 112, 119
   as a kind of aesthetic capital, 122
   in the somatic art of Jackson Pollack, 103
   spontaneity-as-free-will compared with, 120
   syntactic and formal constraints on, 113–114, *114f4.4*
   the true self revealed in (from Confucian and Daoist perspectives), 111
agency
   action syntax as an aspect of effortless attention, 78–79
   phenomenal agency and volition required in thinking of action in the West, 54–55, 98, 132n11
allographic arts, 135n18
Alperson, Philip, on musical improvisation, 94
Aristotle
   concept of *automaton* compared with *ziran*, 17–19
   concept of *hexis* compared with *ziran*, 21–22, *21t1.1*
   concept of *physis* compared with *ziran*, 19–20
   concept of the practical syllogism compared with *ziran*, 22–24

Aristotle *(continued)*
   deliberative thinking favored by, 22, 25, 31, 33, 130n16
   Descartes' use of Christian ideas to revive Plato and Aristotle, 28
   fatalism/determinism as problematic for, 43–44
   internal peace (*eudaimonia*) compared with Daoist sense of ease in the moment, 22
   notion of action compared with *ziran*, 24–25, 25t1.2, 38–39, 64, 112
   On the Motion of Animals, 24
   theory of action that includes responsibility, 55, 64, 112, 130n17
artifice
   the boundaries of nature and artifice, 63–64
   defined as behavior stemming from a Φ-self, 53
   and freedom in Schiller, 32
   in nature, 45–46
   as *wei* 為, 13, 17, 128n7
attention
   ADHD (attention deficit hyperactivity disorder), 87–88, 133n7
   as a kind of psychological capital (according to Csikszentmihalyi), 122, 139–140n51
   paradigm of attention theory in cognitive science, 73–74, 90
   postvoluntary attention identified by Dobrynin, 59–60, 75–76
   training of attention studied by Tang, 78, 89
   See also Stroop task
attention–EFFORTFUL ATTENTION
   of children with ADHD, 87–88
   effort associated with attention by Kahneman, 66, 68–71, 69f3.2, 73
   in the perception-action cycle, 84
   shift from voluntary attention to postvoluntary attention, 59–60
   tied to morality by James, 30–31
attention–EFFORTLESS ATTENTION
   and integrative body-mind training developed by Tang, 88, 89
   of moment-to-moment attention (according to Hommel), 84, 89
   ziran as high attention with low effort, 75, 90
Aunger, Robert, artifice defined by, 46
automaticity
   as an aspect of effortless attention, 78–79
   as a constituent of flow, 76
   of day-to-day activity experienced as effortless, 82, 84
   interruption by the "self-invoking trigger," 80–81, 119

Borg, Gunnar, 72
Borgia, Gerald, 45
Botvinick, Matthew and Joseph T. McGuire, 85–87, 89
bowerbirds, 45–46, 52, 64
Brown, Lee B.
   compositional view of improvisation, 105t4.1, 108, 138n42
   on free jazz performance as improvisation, 106
   retrospective/prospective distinction, 137–138n39

calligraphy / brush writing (*shu* 書)
   Chiang Yee on the art of Chinese calligraphy, 92, 134n11

Chinese calligraphers. *See* Dong Qichang; Huang Tingjian; Wang Xizhi; Zhang Jizhi
  nature as a fundamental inspiration of (according to Chiang Yee), 95–97
  as one of the Confucian six arts (*liu yi* 六藝), 94–95
Carter, Curtis L.
  improvisation in dance viewed as inventive, 105t4.1, 107, 138n42, 139n50
  improvisation viewed as fundamentally derivative, 108
Cézanne
  inventive improvisation by, 107, 109f4.2
  new way of seeing, 106–107
Chiang, Yee
  on the art of Chinese calligraphy, 92, 134n11
  on emotional energy vitalizing artistry, 100
  on nature as the fundamental inspiration of calligraphy, 95–97
Chinese aesthetics
  qi 氣 (energy with materiality), 100–101, 130n19
  qiyun 氣韻 (vitalized by emotional energy), 100
  shen 神 (spirit), 100–101, 130n19, 131n27
Christianity
  Descartes' use of Christian ideas to revive Plato and Aristotle, 28
  formalized movement of Catholic masses, 114
  tianzhu 天主 used to explain the idea of God by Catholic Jesuit missionaries, 7, 128n1
Chrysippus, 26, 31, 130n18
Cochrane, Richard
  on constants and variables in musical performance, 93, 105–106, 105t4.1
  improvisation viewed as fundamentally derivative, 108
  on musical improvisation as musical decision making, 93
cognitive diversity. *See* diversity-COGNITIVE DIVERSITY
cognitive effort. *See* effort-COGNITIVE EFFORT
cognitive sciences
  areas of the brain involved in decision making, 84–85, 85f3.4
  assumptions in the field exposed by introducing the idea of *ziran*, 5, 65, 124
  boundaries in the cognitive science of action and awareness exposed by the case of flow, 63
  effort/attention measured by. *See* attention; attention-EFFORTFUL ATTENTION; attention-EFFORTLESS ATTENTION
  paradigm of attention theory, 73, 90
  philosophers doing conceptual work in, 89, 132n1
  See also Stroop task
cognitive training
  exercises developed for children with ADHD, 88–89
  mental training as an aspect of effortless attention, 78–79
concentration
  as an aspect of aesthetic spontaneity, 102, 103, 112, 117–118
  as an aspect of autotelic experience, 60–61, 97
  as an aspect of Daoist natural action, 15–16, 21–22, 21t1.1, 75

concentration *(continued)*
  as attention, 73, 75, 129n10
  of the cicada catcher in the *Zhuangzi*, 14
  as a psychological aspect of *ziran*, 14, 15, 129n10
Confucius and Confucians
  natural action held as the ideal type of action, 15, 17
  ren 仁 in the *Analects,* 18
  six arts (*liu yi* 六藝), 94–95, 97, 134n9
  ziran understood as revealing the true self, 111
C-self (self-organized systems). *See* self and kinds of self–C-SELF
Csikszentmihalyi, Mihaly
  artists studied by, 61, 98
  on attention as a kind of psychological capital, 122, 139–140n51
  on capital in psychology, 139–140n51
  flow (autotelic experience) described by, 60–61, 76, 97–98
  on flow with respect to positive psychology, 77
  rock climbers interviewed by, 61–62, 98

Danto, Arthur, 123
Daoism
  Aristotle's favoring of deliberative thinking compared with, 130n16
  non-action. *See wu wei* 無為
  spontaneous self-causation. *See* natural action in Daoism
Darwin, Charles, 26, 34
Day, William
  compositional view of improvisation, 105t4.1, 106, 108
  on everyday improvisation, 106, 137n32
decision making
  areas of the brain involved in, 85–86, 85f3.4
  as an aspect of effortless attention, 78–79
  Kahneman on, 66
  musical improvisation as musical decision making, 93
determinism
  Aristotelian, 130n17
  fate and metaphysical, 43
  free will / determinism dichotomy in the Western tradition, 26, 34, 37, 46, 120, 131n5, 135n20
  human action viewed as deterministic by Chrysippus, 26
  in James, 30
  and the paradox of spontaneity, 26–27, 39–40, 64, 135n20
  in physics, 131n4
  in Schiller, 33–34
  stimulus-response determinism exemplified by Pavlov's dogs, 120
diversity, identity diversity, 2–3, 127n1
diversity–COGNITIVE DIVERSITY
  ancient culture as a reservoir of, 4, 134n8
  cultural diversity applied as cognitive diversity, 124–125, 134n8
  defined by Scott Page, 2, 3, 90
  and effective problem solving, 2–3, 4
Dobrynin, Nikolaj
  postvoluntary attention identified by, 59–60, 75–76
  three kinds of attention distinguished by, 59

Dong Qichang 董其昌, calligraphy attributed to, 101, *102*f4.3

ease
  as an aspect of Daoist natural action, 15–16, *21*t1.1
  of the cicada catcher in the *Zhuangzi*, 15
  fluent actions associated with, 75, 121–122
  subjective feeling of ease vs. objective appearance of ease, 103, 136n27
  of the swimmer in the *Zhuangzi*, 15–16
effort
  attention does *not* equal subjective or objective effort, 74, 80, 89
  attention equals effort paradigm, 66–71, 73–74
  ease without strain distinguished from, 121
  effortless attention in relation to, 78–79
  measured in response to demands of a task, 66–67, 67f3.1
  objective effort distinguished from subjective effort, 72
  objective physiological effort, 72, 79–80
  in physics, 133n3
  subjective and objective effort not distinguished by Kahneman, 73
effort–COGNITIVE EFFORT
  objective and subjective effort distinguished, 73, 78
  objective effort in physics compared with, 72–73, 133n3
  pupil dilation associated with, 68
  sympathetic dominance of the autonomic nervous system associated with, 68–70

effortful attention. *See* attention–EFFORTFUL ATTENTION
effortless attention. *See* attention–EFFORTLESS ATTENTION
Effortless Attention (book edited by Bruya)
  Hommel's work on moment-to-moment attention, 84, 89
  McGuire and Botvinick's work on possible neural correlates of flow, 85–87, 89
  restatement and summary in Chapter 3 of, 65–90*passim*, 124
  seven aspects studied in, 78–79
  Wulf's work on how focus of attention affects performance, 80–81
Epicurus, 26, 130n18

Gilmour, John C.
  compositional view of improvisation, 108
  view of improvisation as inventive, *105*t4.1, 107
  view of improvisation away from convention, 106–107, 138n42
Goodman, Nelson, 123, 135n18
Gould, Carol S., and Kenneth Keaton
  on improvisation in classical music, 93, *105*t4.1, 106, 138n39, 138n42
  improvisation viewed as fundamentally derivative, 108, 109
Gowers, Timothy, 1
Graham, A. C., on skill stories in the *Zhuangzi* referred to as knack stories, 128n8
Greek language and philosophy
  Western way of thinking rooted in, 4, 25, 43

Greek language and philosophy *(continued)*
  word choice challenges in comparing Chinese ideas with Greek ideas, 18–19
  See also Aristotle; Chrysippus; Epicurus; Plato
Greenberg, Clement, 111

Hofmann, Hans, 103
Hommel, Bernhard
  normal attention identified as largely effortless, 82, 84, 89
  perception-action cycle described by, 81–82, *83*f3.3, 84
Hong, Lu, 2, 90
Huang Tingjian 黄庭坚 (Northern Song calligrapher), 92, *93*f4.1, 100–101
hypnosis and hypnotic suggestion, 56–58, 62

improvisation–perspectives, 92–94, *105*t4.1
  Brown on situated, impromptu, unscripted improvisation, *105*t4.1, 106
  Brown's retrospective/prospective distinction, 137–138n39
  Carter's inventive perspective, *105*t4.1, 107, 108, 138n42, 139n50
  class of derivative improvisation, 108–110, *109*t4.2, 137–138n39
  class of wholesale composition, 108–109, *109*t4.2, 137n38
  Gould and Keaton's interpretive perspective on classical music, 93, *105*t4.1, 106, 108, 109, 138n39, 138n42
  Young and Matheson on the indeterminacy of structural properties, 92, 105, *105*t4.1
  See also Brown, Lee B.; Cochrane, Richard; Day, William; Gilmour, John C.; Sawyer, R. Keith; Sterritt, David; Young, James O. and Carl Matheson
interference
  movement achieved in *ziran* without external interference, 11, 16, 38, 74
  and the paradox of *spontaneity*, 39–40
interference effect. *See* Stroop task

James, William, 30–31, 34

Kahneman, Daniel
  Attention and Effort by, 66, 71, 133n2
  attention equals effort theory of, 66–71, 78
  measurement of attention/effort, 68–70, *69*f3.2
  physiological vs. cognitive effort not distinguished by, 79
  subjective and objective effort not distinguished by, 73
Kandinsky, Wassily, 139n45
Kant, Immanuel
  contingent/necessary dichotomy adopted by Schiller, 31
  distinction between regulative and constitutive principles, 139n47
  model of a dignified person, 32–33
  paradox of spontaneity in relation to his aesthetic theory, 135n20
Karlgren, Bernard, 95
Keaton, Kenneth. *See* Gould, Carol S., and Kenneth Keaton
Kernfeld, Barry, 138n41
Kerouac, Jack, writing process, 110–111, 138n43, 139n44
Kourlas, Gia, on Paul Taylor's dance company, 100
Krasner, Lee, 103, 136n24

La Mettrie, Julian Offray de, 27–28
Laozi 老子, 8
  pronunciation of, 128n3
Laozi
  Aristotle's view of action
    compared with, 20, 21, 24
  the character *ran* 然 in, 8
  the character *zi* 自 in, 8–11
  contemporary character of Laozi's
    naturalistic assumptions, 34–35
  La Mettrie's view of action
    compared with, 27
  notion of *ziran* in, 8–11, 74
  Rousseau's view of action
    compared with, 28, 29
  Schiller's views of a action
    compared with, 33
  wu wei in passages from, 12–13
Ledderose, Lothar, 99
letting go
  Aristotle's concept of *hexis*
    compared with, 21–22, 21t1.1
  as an aspect of Daoist natural
    action, 15–16, 21t1.1
  as part of Pollock's aesthetic
    spontaneity, 103
  in the skill stories in the
    Zhuangzi, 13–16, 75, 118–119
  tree stump that has lost awareness
    (*jue* 橛), 119, 139n48

Macaulay, Alastair, on Mark Morris,
  99
McGuire, Joseph T. and Matthew M.
  Botvinick, 85–87, 89
Matheson, Carl. *See* Young, James
  O., and Carl Matheson

Naccache, Lionel, 73
natural action in Daoism
  concentration as an aspect of. *See*
    concentration
  ease as an aspect of. *See* ease

  four aspects of aesthetic
    spontaneity, 103, 107, 112
  four aspects of summarized,
    14–16
  as the ideal type of action, 16–17,
    21t1.1, 25t1.2, 39, 39t2.1, 74, 75
  letting go as an aspect of. *See*
    letting go
  responsiveness as an aspect of. *See*
    responsiveness
  wu wei as a term for. *See wu wei*
    無為
  ziran as a blanket term for, 7
  See also spontaneity; *ziran*
natural action as a descriptor for
  action and movement
  aesthetic appreciation of, 42–43
  Aristotelian ideal action compared
    with, 24–25, 39
  Aristotelian *physis* compared with,
    19–20
  artifice in relation to, 46, 53,
    134n12
  behavior under hypnosis and, 56–58
  from Chinese thought, 7, 38
  in early China, 17
  flow and, 59–63
  as an ideal in achievement, 14, 17,
    19, 97, 99–100, 136n27
  as impossible to apply to human
    action, 43–46, 64
  in La Mettrie, 27–28
  of movement in nature, 17
  in the paradox of spontaneity,
    26–27, 40, 64
  in Rousseau's conception of God,
    29–30
  in Schiller, 32–34, 32t1.3
  self-organization and, 47–63
  sleep-walking behavior and, 55–56
  as translation of *ziran*, 12
natural as a descriptor for human
  beings, 44–45, 63, 129n10

nature and movement
  and aesthetics, 41–43
  associated with Chinese art, 95–97, 134n12
  self-organized motion in plants, 37, 50, 132n9
  in Western philosophy. *See* paradox of spontaneity; philosophy of action
  wu wei defined as action that is absent direct intentionality, 12, 13
  ziran used to refer to motion in nature broadly, 13

Page, Scott, 2–3, 90
paradox of spontaneity
  contradictory accounts of movement in Western philosophy of action, 26–27, 40, 64
  in Kant, 135n20
  relation to natural human action as theoretically impossible, 64
  resolved, 64
Φ-self (phenomenal self). *See* self and kinds of self–Φ-SELF (PHENOMENAL SELF)
philosophy
  of action. *See* philosophy of action
  of art, *See* aesthetics; aesthetic spontaneity
  comparative philosophy, 5, 18, 123–125, 127n2
  and the contribution of ancient insights to intellectual endeavors today, 4
  Greek. *See* Greek language and philosophy
philosophy of action
  Aristotle *On the Motion of Animals*, 23–24
  Aristotle's theory of action compared with *ziran,* 24–25, 25t1.2, 38–39, 64, 112
  Aristotle's theory of action that includes responsibility, 24–25, 25t1.2, 55, 64, 112, 130n17
  contradictory accounts of spontaneity. *See* paradox of spontaneity
  definition of, 38
  human action viewed as deterministic by Chrysippus, 26
  natural human action viewed as impossible, 44–45
  persistence of Western ideas about, 34
  Schiller's necessity and contingency dichotomy, 31–34, 32t1.3
  volition's role in, 54, 63–64
  See also natural action in Daoism; *natural action* as a descriptor for action and movement
Picasso, Sawyer on his process of painting, 104, 105t4.1, 109, 109t4.2, 136–137n30, 138n42
Plato
  Aristotelian concepts of nature contrasted with, 130n17
  Descartes' use of Christian ideas to revive Plato and Aristotle, 28
  Whitehead on Plato's importance to Western philosophy, 25
Pollack, Jackson
  aesthetic spontaneity achieved by, 103
  emotional energy of his action in creating paintings, 136n24
Posner, Michael
  children with ADHD studied by, 87–88

effortful control studied by, 87,
88–89
postvoluntary attention, 59–60, 73,
75–76
Prablanc, C., and D. Pélisson, 82

qi 氣 (a kind of energy that also
possesses materiality)
defined as an inner rhythm, 100
as a mark of excellence, 100, 111
metaphysical continuity with the
material world, 130n19, 131n27

Raz, Amir and Natasha K. J.
Campbell, 132n13
Raz, Amir, Jin Fan, and Michael I.
Posner, 132n13
responsiveness
as a characteristic of aesthetic
spontaneity, 119–120
concentration and letting go
related to, 102–103, 119
deliberation contrasted with, 25,
130n16
fluent actions associated with,
75
as a psychological aspect of
ziran / natural action in
Daoism, 15–16, 21t1.1, 22, 28,
119, 130n16
in relation to syntactic constraints
in the martial arts, 114
sensitivity and, 28, 103, 120–121
of the swimmer in the *Zhuangzi*,
15
Rothbart, Mary, 87
Rousseau, Jean-Jacques
ideal of the noble savage, 28, 29,
32
mistrust of rationality, 29, 32
unification of matter and spirit
compared with *ziran*, 29–30

Sawyer, R. Keith
compositional view of improvisation,
92, 104–106, *105*t4.1, 108, 109,
136–137n30, 137n38
on Picasso's process of painting,
104, 109, *109*t4.2, 136–137n30,
138n42
Schiller, Friedrich
model of a graceful person, 32–33
necessity and contingency
dichotomy, 31–34, *32*t1.3
notion of spontaneity in grace,
135n20
science and the scientific method
of cognition. *See* cognitive
sciences
effective problem solving in, 1–3
habits of thinking of various
disciplines of, 3–4
laws of nature emphasized during
the Enlightenment, 43
self-organized motion in plants,
37, 50, 132n9
Searle, John R., 139n47
self and kinds of self, 52t2.3
use of the prefix *self-* to get a
purchase on our metaphysics,
48–51, 131–132n8
self and kinds of self–C-SELF, 52t2.3,
55–59
defined as a self-organizing
complex, 52
natural action associated with, 53,
58, 63
persistent quality of, 52–53
psychological states of C-self
dominance, 59, 61–63
self and kinds of self–Φ-SELF
(PHENOMENAL SELF)
artifice associated with, 53
consciousness and self-awareness
associated with, 52, 58

self and kinds of self–Φ-SELF
(PHENOMENAL SELF) *(continued)*
defined as a single kind of self, 52, 53–54
during autotelic experiences of flow, 61–62
impact of hypnosis on, 58, 62
intermittent quality of, 53–54
psychological states of Φ-self deficit, 59
shen 神 (often translated as spirit or god)
as a mark of excellence, 100–101, 103, 136n24
metaphysical continuity with the material world, 130n19, 131n27
Shusterman, Richard, idea of somaesthetics, 134n17
somatic arts
aesthetic spontaneity as a distinguishing mark of artistry in, 103–104, 111
defined, 99
emotional energy as a term in, 136n24
fluidity of, 99–100
Kerouac's writing as, 110–111
movements of the artist visible in the art product, 99–100
somaesthetics related to, 134n17
spontaneity
aesthetic. *See* aesthetic spontaneity
automaton and, 18–19
Kandinsky's discussion of improvisation, 139n45
La Mettrie's theory of human action, 27–28
paradox of. *See* paradox of spontaneity
as a potential equivalent of *ziran* in the West, 39–40, 74
Sterritt on improvisation, 111

Sterritt, David
authenticity, spontaneity, individuality emphasized by, 105t4.1, 107
spontaneity exemplified by Kerouac's writing process, 111, 138n43, 139n44
Stroop task
attention tested by, 57, 70, 87
facilitation effect, 57–58, 132n13
interference effect, 57–58

Tang, Yiyuan
effortless attention studied by, 78, 87
integrative body-mind training method of meditation practice, 88, 89
Tao, Terence, 1
tian 天 (heaven and nature)
incompatibility with Western metaphysics, 128–129n9
relation to skill stories in the *Zhuangzi*, 14
in *tianzhu* 天主, 7, 128n1

Wang Xizhi 王羲之 and Wang Xianzhi 王獻之, calligraphy by Dong Qichang based on, 101, 102f4.3
Whitehead, Alfred North, on Plato's importance to Western philosophy, 25
Wulf, Gabriel
"self-invoking trigger" phenomenon identified by, 80–81, 119
work on external focus of attention, 79–80, 89
wu wei 無為
concentration as a psychological aspect of, 14

defined, 13, 74–75, 128n7
in the *Laozi,* 12–13
responsiveness as a psychological aspect of, 15
as a term for natural action in the classical Chinese tradition, 7, 16, 74
in terms of leadership, 13
in the *Zhuangzi,* 13–16
ziran related to, 12–16
See also concentration; letting go; nature and movement; *ziran*

Xie He 謝赫, 100

Young, James O., and Carl Matheson
improvisation viewed as fundamentally derivative, 108
improvisation viewed as substitutive, elaborative, completive, 92, 105, *105*t4.1
Yueda, M. R., 87
yun 韻
as a mark of excellence, 100, 101, 103
in *qiyun* 氣韻, 100

Zhang Jizhi 張即之, calligraphy attributed to, 101, *101*f4.2
Zhuangzi, 8
pronunciation of, 128n3
Zhuangzi 莊子
the character *zi* 自 in, 9, 11
contemporary character of Zhuangzi's naturalistic assumptions, 34–35
mind referred to as dead ash, 119, 139n48
as a skeptic about convention, 129n11
Zhuangzi-SKILL STORIES
bell stand carpenter story in, 14–15, 21, 118–119, 121
cicada catcher story in, 14, 15, 21, 22, 31, 118–119, 121
Daoist natural action illustrated in, 13–16
referred to as knack stories by Graham, 128n8
swimmer stories, 15, 21, 25, 31, 39, 119, 121
wholeness and fluency of *ziran* illustrated in, 16, 75
ziran 自然
action arising from internal resources without external interference, 11, 16, 38, 74
as aesthetic spontaneity, 111
application to current theory, 5, 34–35, 40, 65, 89–90, 127n2
and Aristotle. *See ziran* 自然- ARISTOTELIAN CONCEPTS COMPARED WITH
attention and, 129n10
autopoiesis proposed by Maturana and Verala, 12
as a blanket term for natural action. *See* natural action
as central to the creation and evaluation of the arts in China, 96–97
the character *ran* 然 in the *Laozi,* 8
the character *zi* 自 in the *Laozi,* 8–11
the character *zi* 自 in the *Zhuangzi,* 9, 11
Chinese art and aesthetics and, 91–92, 94, 96
in Daoism, 4
as high attention with low effort, 75, 90
as the ideal type of action in Daoism, 17, *21*t1.1, *25*t1.2, 39, *39*t2.1, 74, 75, 129n11

ziran 自然 *(continued)*
   ideal type of action in Daoism associated with. *See* concentration; ease; letting go; natural action in Daoism; responsiveness
   improvisation and, 92–94, 104
   multivalent causation of, 10–11, 16, 38, 74
   as nature, 8, 12
   pronunciation of, 128n2
   Rousseau's unification of matter and spirit compared with, 29–30
   Schiller's concept of grace compared with, 33–34, 135n20
   as self-causation, 11
   somatic art and, 103–104
   as something happening of its own accord, 11, 13, 24, 28, 40, 62, 74
   as spontaneity, 7–12, 18, 39–40, 74, 94, 96
   uniqueness of the idea of *ziran*, 4–5, 19, 65
   Western philosophical ideas distinguished from, 4
   wholeness and fluency of, 75
   wu wei related to, 12–16
ziran 自然–Aristotelian concepts compared with
   automaton in Aristotle distinguished from *ziran*, 17–19
   hexis compared with, 21–22, 21t1.1
   notion of action, 24–25, 25t1.2, 38–39, 64, 112
   physis compared with, 19–20
   practical syllogism distinguished from, 22–24

www.ingramcontent.com/pod-product-compliance
Ingram Content Group UK Ltd.
Pitfield, Milton Keynes, MK11 3LW, UK
UKHW041919140426
5217IPUK00013B/235